# Singing
# and
# Voice Science

# SINGING AND VOICE SCIENCE

**Jean Callaghan**

*Illustrations by Richard Collins*

**Singular Publishing Group**
**Thomson Learning**
401 West A Street, Suite 325
San Diego, California 92101-7904

**Singular Publishing Group,** publishes textbooks, clinical manuals, clinical reference books, journals, videos, and multimedia materials on speech-language pathology, audiology, otorhinolaryngology, special education, early childhood, aging, occupational therapy, physical therapy, rehabilitation, counseling, mental health, and voice. For your convenience, our entire catalog can be accessed on our website at http://www.singpub.com. Our mission to provide you with materials to meet the daily challenges of the ever-changing health care/educational environment will remain on course if we are in touch with you. In that spirit, we welcome your feedback on our products. Please telephone **(1-800-521-8545)**, fax **(1-800-774-8398)**, or e-mail (singpub@singpub.com) your comments and requests to us.

Typeset in 10/12 Palatino by Flanagan's Publishing Services, Inc.
Printed in Canada by Transcontinental Printing.

**Library of Congress Cataloging-in-Publication Data**
Callaghan, Jean.
    Singing and voice science / by Jean Callaghan;
illustrations by Richard Collins.
        p.   cm.
    Includes bibliographical references and index.
    ISBN 0-7693-0044-8 (softcover: alk. paper)
    1. Voice.   2. Singing—Instructions and study.   I. Title.
MT821.C25   1999
783—dc21                                                    99-40616
                                                                CIP

# CONTENTS

# PREFACE

When I began teaching singing 25 years ago, I asked myself such questions as, "How is teaching singing different from singing?" and "What is the accepted body of knowledge about singing?" As a student I had experienced the rival claims that different teachers made about how to manage the breath, how to achieve ideal resonance, and so on, knowledge that they had gradually acquired through their own singing and through years of teaching, listening, and observing. Although I knew from experience what worked best for me as a singer, I had no way of knowing whether what worked for me would also work for students of different voice types, who possess different physiques and different personalities. I was also conscious of the gap between being able to do something and being able to teach someone else to do it. I felt that while an experiential knowledge of the act of singing was important for teaching, so, too, was an understanding of how the voice works physically, of how it operates as a musical instrument, and of how these kinds of knowledge are best conveyed to students.

I knew that although the oboe, like the voice, is a wind instrument, most oboe teachers do not feel the need to investigate in any detail how the oboe is constructed and operates. Some teachers who are curious about such things may do so, but the majority achieve success by being expert players, by knowing the repertoire of the instrument, and by having an intuitive awareness of learning styles. However, the oboe is an object that can be held at arm's length and examined. The oboist can observe the instrument as a whole or take it apart and examine the different parts and how they fit together; the reed can be removed, and the effect on the sound of different reeds and different breath pressures can be observed. In contrast, the voice as an instrument consists of many parts of the singer that are normally hidden from the performer's view and consciousness, which must be assembled at will—and in different conditions—to meet the instrumental demands of music making. The player and the instrument are one.

When I began teaching, I embarked on a critical assessment of the literature on singing and the teaching of singing and found a body of knowledge going back to the 17th century. Much of that literature reflects the fact that player and instrument are one: The singer or singing-teacher author makes no distinction between the knowledge of voice and the practice of teaching. Twenty-five years later, questions about current knowledge of the singing voice have taken on a somewhat different aspect. Scientific knowledge of vocal function and vocal health has increased greatly; new technology can display the larynx in operation, measure muscular effort, and acoustically analyze vocal sound. In a sense, it is now possible to take the objective approach of the oboist, to examine the singer's "reed" and the effect of different breath pressures. Yet my investigations into Australian singing teachers' knowledge of this area (Callaghan, 1998) found that while practitioners demonstrated an admirable commitment to experiential learning and to individual students' development, their knowledge of vocal physiology, acoustics, and health was often incomplete at best and misinformed at worst.

This book addresses the need of those working with the singing voice to add to their armory the relevant knowledge voice science is accumulating. It is a book more about what is taught (voice), than how it is taught (pedagogy). It identifies issues of physiology, acoustics, and health that are pertinent to singing pedagogy and examines scientific understandings of voice relevant to those issues. The book focuses on the vocal technique of the adult voice in singing, with an emphasis on "classical" style. It draws on material published in English over the last 25 years, a period marked by technological innovation and the beginnings of interdisciplinary collaboration and cross-disciplinary communication.

The first chapter outlines the long oral tradition of voice teaching that began in Italy early in the 17th century, 19th century changes, and the new information on voice available in our own time. Chapter 2 gives an overview of the vocal instrument, that is the body, drawing a distinction between two essentially different ways of observing and understanding the body. One is the first-person perspective of the singer, the other the third-person perspective of the scientist. Both types of knowledge are necessary for the teacher of singing. This overview provides the background to Chapters 3 through 7, which comprise an exploration of aspects of singing that have been investigated by science. Scientific studies are assessed and related to practitioner understandings to provide the knowledge necessary for teachers. Chapter 3 deals with breath management,

Chapter 4 with phonation, Chapter 5 with resonance and articulation, Chapter 6 with registration, and Chapter 7 with vocal health. These threads are drawn together in Chapter 8, which relates the specific physical aspects of vocal technique to the pedagogical concern with overall control of the instrument and makes recommendations for the professional education of singing teachers.

I hope that this account of the current state of voice science as it relates to singing will prove useful to singing teachers who, as I did 25 years ago, wish to find out all they can about the workings of that superb musical instrument, the human voice.

# ACKNOWLEDGMENTS

My thanks go to the singing teachers—in Sydney, Perth and London —who have taught me at different stages of my career. My thanks also go to the many colleagues and students who have stimulated my interest in voice. It was Richard Miller who first suggested that my doctoral research might form the basis of a book; I am grateful to him for that suggestion and to Alison Winkworth for her enthusiasm about the book when it was little more than an idea.

I am delighted with Richard Collins' entertaining illustrations and grateful to Bruce Petty for his permission to reproduce drawings originally displayed at the Powerhouse Museum, Sydney.

I am grateful to the University of Western Sydney, Nepean, for supporting this work through a Publications Time Release Scholarship.

And again I thank John, who is there in the background providing support, humor and practical help, and only offers criticism when I invite it.

*To Ruth and Kate, with love and admiration*

# C H A P T E R

# 1

# *Science and Singing*

*A knowledge of the voice is necessary for everyone, but above all this is necessary for a teacher of singing.*

(Bérard, 1755/1969, pp. 61–62)

## The Oral Tradition of Bel Canto

Current knowledge about the singing voice exists against the background of a long oral tradition. That tradition grew out of the approach to voice teaching of the bel canto period, beginning in Italy early in the 17th century. This approach represents the foundation of singing pedagogy in the Western European art tradition.

Through three centuries of cultural and musical change, the initial precepts and specific practices of bel canto have been so modified that bel canto can no longer be said to exist. A multiplicity of tonal ideals and corresponding pedagogical practices have evolved in different national schools (Miller, 1997), and it may be that multicultural societies such as Australia, New Zealand, Canada, and the United States embrace a range of ideals and practices. Nevertheless, bel canto ideals and the bel canto approach to teaching live on in writings on singing technique—even in writings directed to different national schools, to vocal technique for repertoire far removed from the repertoire of bel canto, and in scientifically based writings. Similarly, practitioners continue in the master-apprentice tradition of bel canto, using exercises and technical directives passed on from teacher to pupil over centuries. Because of the profound, pervasive, and

I

continuing influence of the bel canto teaching tradition on singing pedagogy and vocal knowledge, I will begin with an examination of that tradition and of the forces that have made it no longer the complete and self-sufficient model for singing pedagogy that it once was.

The history of the development of bel canto has been well documented, both by general music historians (Bukofzer, 1947; Palisca, 1968; Weaver, 1980) and by writers with a more particular interest in singing (Heriot, 1956; Galliver, 1974; Manén, 1987; Celetti, 1991). Bibliographical surveys of bel canto sources have also been undertaken (e.g., Duey, 1951).

The teaching of singing as a solo virtuoso art goes back to early 17th-century Italy, where it developed in response to the demand for solo vocal virtuosos to sing the new monody and opera. While the poet-lutenist-singer had been a familiar entertainer at courts throughout the Renaissance, he was not primarily a vocal virtuoso. Palisca (1968) quoted a contemporary witness as observing that the solo professional singer began to emerge as an important figure in musical life around 1570. At around the same time, society was giving increasing attention to emotional expression and the cultivation of virtuosity. With the development of opera came the training to meet these demands.

The 17th- and 18th-century tradition of bel canto was based on the continuity of objectives, of technique, and of criteria for musical judgment; it was also dependent on the close relationship between composer and performer, teacher and student, performer and audience. The teacher (who was often also a composer) was an accomplished performer in the musical style who acted as an example to the student. The student practiced assiduously and, by trial and error, eventually produced the approved sound, learned what sensations accompanied production of that sound, and thus learned how to reproduce it.

## The Teaching of the Bel Canto Masters

The bel canto tradition has been largely an oral one, which presents obvious—perhaps insuperable—problems to 20th-century historians aiming to document the practice of the 17th and 18th centuries. There are no recordings of 17th-century vocal sound, and the technical teaching of the singing studio can be deduced only from the writings of singers and teachers, published technical exercises, and the repertoire for which singers were training.

The primary aim of voice teaching was to produce "beautiful" tone and agility, allied to a sensitive ear. Singers cultivated good

breath control for the singing of extended phrases. Voice teachers taught techniques (musical as much as vocal) for emotionally expressive singing and for vocal ornamentation. The tradition emphasized the natural abilities of the pupil and the obligation of the teacher to develop these abilities. The singing experience of the teacher was the most important component of the process, and teaching proceeded by example on the part of the master and repeated trial and error on the part of the pupil.

> In giving the precise rules to a student let the teacher not only tell him and explain to him, but let him illustrate his meaning by making himself an example. . . . Let the experienced teacher follow this method and he will soon be convinced how much more preferable are practical demonstrations to general rules. (Mancini, 1774/1777/1967, p. 103)

In keeping with the new status of the singer as virtuoso, an understanding of the vocal instrument was expected. In Italy, Tosi (1743/1987, p. x) advocated "a little less Fiddling with the Voice, and a little more Singing with the Instrument." In France, Bérard asserted that:

> A singer who does profound research on the mechanism of the voice will have a great facility in forming high and low sounds. He will command his organs in any way, he will hasten or retard their movement according to his convenience. He will draw from them strong, vigorous, and mellow sounds, as well as tender, light, and mannered sounds. (1755/1969, p. 61)

Many writers emphasized the obligations of the teacher. Tosi, for example, wrote:

> let him hear with a disinterested ear whether the person desirous to learn has a voice and a disposition, that he may not be obliged to give a strict account to God of the parent's money ill spent, and the injury done to the child by the irreparable loss of time, which might have been more profitably employed in some other profession. (1743/1987, p. 2)

There was an emphasis on the natural gifts expected of the singing student: a pleasing appearance; adequate breathing capacity; no malformation of face, mouth, or body; and a good ear. Posture and facial expression were to be "graceful" or "natural." A positive mental attitude, both in study and performance, was advocated. Most of the old masters were interested primarily in breath management and the ability to sing extended phrases. Many of the Italian sources contain rules where the performer may breathe in long passages and give hints about cutting some notes short in order to obtain needed breath (Duey, 1951).

Theories of phonation were based on incomplete or incorrect information. The anatomy of the throat was well understood for all practical purposes, but the physiology of the vocal organs was not, nor is it yet. While some writers presented simplified, and often incorrect, descriptions or diagrams of the vocal organs, these seem to have little to do with their descriptions of vocal technique. Singers made no attempt at conscious control of particular muscles. Instead, teachers urged the singer to keep a natural and free muscular balance of all physical faculties in order for the body to respond naturally and quickly to the sense and idea of both text and music. Blanchet was unusual in advocating conscious muscular control of the larynx, and significantly, he was not a musician (Duey, 1951).

Teachers gave directions on resonance that were linked to the coordination of respiration and sound production. Singers were concerned with keeping the voice free and producing it orally rather than nasally. The great masters spoke of "opening the throat," "loosening the neck," and "singing the tone forward, at the lips." Many wrote of the different qualities and emotional effects of particular vowels.

All of the early writers had something to say about the registers of the voice and how they should be blended. Unfortunately, because these writers formed a great deal of their opinions by observing castrati, the information is now difficult to interpret. Registers were named according to the singer's sensations of sympathetic vibration, for example, the chest or head registers. There is some confusion for modern readers in the use of the term "falsetto," which may refer to either what other writers call "head" or to the lighter, breathier tone of the male voice above its full-toned "head" range. (Register terminology is examined in detail in Chapter 6.)

The earliest Italian writers, such as Caccini (1602/1970), did not advocate use of the head voice. This may be because they wrote for a male public and also because of the narrow range demanded by the early declamatory style. Later writers such as Tosi and Mancini considered the head voice to be an essential quality and the blending of chest and head voice to be vital before attempting to acquire agility.

Writers stressed the importance of a good ear and the necessity for precise intonation. It was assumed that the teacher had a good enough ear and sufficient singing experience to be able to identify and correct faults of intonation or tone. The masters generally agreed that moderation in eating, drinking, and living was important to vocal health. Vocal strain was to be avoided to preserve the voice.

Bel canto developed and flourished within the context of a particular musical style that dominated art music in Italy and many other parts of Europe for over two centuries. Notwithstanding changes and developments within that style, there was little serious disagreement among practitioners from the early 17th century until the early 19th century about the musical function of the singing voice or about what constituted good singing. This musical style formed the accepted context for the teaching of bel canto singing.

Likewise, there was only one model for the teaching of bel canto singing. Because the masters generally agreed on the broad precepts of singing and on the means by which these ends were to be reached, the approach was a direct and simple one, conveyed in a master-apprentice relationship. The bel canto masters taught one-on-one, apprenticeship-style: The teacher gave instructions and set an example, while the student attempted to follow the master's advice, emulate the master's results, and over time perhaps achieve master's status.

Over the last 150 years or so, the musical and social assumptions underlying this model for the teaching of singing have ceased to be self-evident. Some of the factors underlying this change are discussed in the rest of this chapter.

## New Uses of the Singing Voice

Many musical developments from the late 18th century and during the 19th century contributed to different, heavier demands on singers. Public concerts meant larger venues, gave increasing importance to the conductor, and contributed to the separation of the roles of composer, performer, and teacher.

During the 18th century, the functions of voice and orchestra in opera had been clearly defined: The orchestra accompanied the singers and played by itself only on specified occasions. The 19th-century desire to blur boundaries led to use of the orchestra not only to create mood but also to enter into the drama as a continuous web of instrumental sound. In the late works of Verdi, for example, the voices compete with a large orchestra employed as part of the drama. With increasingly chromatic music, the orchestra grew in size and importance, culminating in Wagner's music dramas, in which the orchestra develops the entire action while the voice declaims in melody strictly molded to the text. These lengthy works, and later the operas of Puccini and the works for voice and orchestra of Mahler and Strauss, all called for hitherto-unimagined vocal and physical stamina.

## Science and Singing

The Spanish singer Manuel Garcia (1805–1906) is a legendary figure in vocal pedagogy and voice research. His studies in Naples with Ansani provided him with links to the bel canto traditions of Porpora.

His studies in France with his father exposed him to the new style of singing introduced into France by the tenor Duprez in 1837 (Paschke, 1975). His own vocal problems motivated him to invent the laryngoscope, a mirror apparatus used to view the larynx with the intention of showing how it produced sounds and registers (Garcia, 1894/1982). (The laryngoscope is still often used by doctors to view the larynx.)

Garcia had the idea that bel canto was produced by vibrations of the vocal cords only, caused by a full breath propelled by a bellows-like action of the muscles of the chest, forcing air from the lungs through the vocal cords (coup de glotte). On the foundation of his vocal-cord theory, Garcia built up a method for the training of singers, published in 1840 under the title of *L'Art du chant*. In 1856, he published a revised version of this manual, called *Nouveau Traité de l'art du chant*, which became a standard text.

Garcia's development of a method of teaching based on his experimental investigations reflects the growth and increasing importance of the natural sciences in the 19th century. However, his emphasis on the vocal folds and on the separate elements of the vocal mechanism failed to explain their interdependent working. Although his work represented an important advance in scientific knowledge about the voice, it also represented the beginning of fragmentation of knowledge about vocal technique.

The serious attempts at scientific study of the voice continued into the 20th century. Garcia's work was continued by his pupil Mathilde Marchesi (1901; n.d.). A scientific stance is also apparent in Emma Seiler's *The Voice in Singing* (1890). Seiler, a pupil of the German acoustician and physiologist Helmholtz, taught singing in America. She advocated study not only of the aesthetic side of the art of singing, but of the "physiological and physical side also, without an exact knowledge, appreciation, observance, and study of which, what is hurtful cannot be discerned and avoided" (p. 34).

Nonetheless, voice science and vocal pedagogy remained independent of each other, despite such attempts to bring them together. Works describing the mechanism, usually by doctors or physiologists, often emphasized how to avoid vocal problems. Works by singer-teachers more often described the singer's sensations when producing particular sounds, and espoused "correct" methods for producing "good" sound. Rarely did the two approaches meet. This division has persisted almost to the present day.

Since the 1960s, works attempting to integrate the scientific and the experiential, written by singers with scientific interests or doctors and physiologists interested in singing, have become more common. Some of these works are discussed later in this book.

## Contemporary Voice Science

Modern voice science and vocal pedagogy are products of the last 30 years or so. In that period, voice science has been transformed by new technologies that can view the larynx in operation, measure muscular effort, and provide real-time feedback on vocal acoustics. That period has also seen the emergence of interdisciplinary collaboration between voice specialists in research, clinical, and performance disciplines. Interdisciplinary collaboration and the use of new technologies have raised new questions for voice research, and the answers are leading to a better understanding of how the vocal instrument works and how its health can be maintained. Voice science is both increasing our understanding of the ways in which the performer's voice may most efficiently be employed and in some areas confirming the wisdom of traditional pedagogies.

## Science for Singing Teachers

The tradition of vocal pedagogy has been largely an oral one. This tradition continues into the 20th century despite a breakdown in many of the social and musical assumptions that previously underpinned it and despite the pressures of modern mass education. Today many of the larger concerns of a rapidly changing society impact the field of singing pedagogy: science vs. art, elitism vs. populism, the national vs. the international, the rational vs. the instinctive.

While many of the precepts of the bel canto masters, based on observation and experience, have largely been proven sound by scientific investigation, such a "natural," slow, and generalized approach to the teaching of vocal technique in singing is no longer adequate. The range of vocal styles current at the end of the 20th century means that teachers may need to teach students who wish to train as professional performers in a vocal tradition other than the teacher's own or to sing for self-expression and amateur music making. Moreover, the human voice remains the most convenient, portable musical instrument for use in music education and group music making at all levels (Atterbury & Richardson, 1995; Durrant & Welch, 1995). To achieve maximum results in minimum time and without vocal strain, a knowledge of vocal technique is useful to music educator and choral director (Phillips, 1992; Miller, 1995). Most teachers need to work with students of voice types other than their own. Perhaps even more than in Tosi's day, teachers—particularly in postcompulsory education—are required to give strict account of the time and money spent in training singers.

To meet these demands requires an understanding of the combination of physical factors that safely and efficiently produces the appropriate vocal sound. It is no longer adequate for practitioners to base their teaching solely on the directives that were used in their own training, on techniques they have heard used by famous singers in master classes, or on the personal imagery that has worked for them in their own singing regardless of whether these directives are well based in physical function and vocal acoustics and whether such images suggest the appropriate coordinations to the student. Such an approach may be inefficient or ineffective; it may also be deficient in imparting some essential skills, such as those needed to prevent vocal damage.

In the last 25 years, a great deal of scientific material has been published on various aspects of vocal physiology and acoustics. This evidence is scattered through journals in many different disciplines—physiology, medicine, speech pathology, acoustics, and linguistics, as well as singing and voice science—contributing to the fragmentation of knowledge on voice.

All of these factors—the disruption of a continuous single tradition of vocal pedagogy, the proliferation of vocal styles, the heavy physical demands of singing with electronic instruments or large orchestras in large spaces, fragmentation of sources of knowledge about voice, and new information about vocal function and vocal health—have contributed to a state of some confusion in vocal pedagogy.

This confusion was recognized as early as 1947, when Victor Alexander Fields, in *Training the Singing Voice*, wrote of "confusion in the vocal teaching profession" (p. 3), and the need to give a pedagogical interpretation to scientific discoveries about the singing voice. In 1947, Fields isolated a difficulty in singing pedagogy that has since continued to grow and become even more significant:

> The laboratory research worker is often far removed in his thinking from the teaching practices of the classroom or studio. Conversely, the singing teacher often must handle unpredictable personality problems with intuitive insight and improvised instructional techniques that are not readily amenable to experimental analysis. (p. 15)

Fields' book essayed a reconciliation of these points of view through analysis of the working concepts of singing pedagogy embodied in works published in the period from 1928 to 1941. He commented that, while there was no lack of printed material on the subjects of singing and voice culture, this material is inaccessible to teachers because it is extremely diversified and fragmentary and diffusely distributed throughout a variety of books, periodicals, scientific papers, reports of experiments, and published interviews that have never been correlated from the standpoint of a definite vocal pedagogy. His statement that "what is written about the singing voice is so often overlaid and interwoven with conflicting theories and extravagant conjectures that misinterpretations are inevitable" (1947, p. 1) pointed to the gap between scientific reports and writings by practitioners. He went on to summarize a mass of critical comment, outlining 21 different categories of complaint voiced by authors, to support his claim that the field of vocal pedagogy stood badly in need of clarification. Fields' aims were to survey and correlate available sources of bibliographic information on methods of training the singing voice in order to provide both a core of organized information for the use of singing teachers and an orientation for research in the field. His bibliographic survey covered pedagogy, breathing, phonation, resonance, range, dynamics, ear training, diction, and interpretation.

Another landmark in 20th-century writings on singing technique, William Vennard's *Singing: The Mechanism and the Technic*, was published in 1949—2 years after Fields' book—and revised and greatly enlarged in 1967. Like Fields, Vennard was concerned with relating aspects of singing pedagogy to the acoustic, anatomical, and physiological facts of voice, but his work is a textbook for teachers and singers rather than a bibliographic survey.

In the nearly 20 years between Vennard's first and second editions, scientific investigation of singing voice grew rapidly. In both editions, Vennard stated his aim as "to compile under one cover objective findings from various reliable sources and to relate them to the art of singing" (1967, p. iii) and went on to hint at the same difficulties that Fields had articulated:

> As the title indicates, this book is frankly mechanistic. . . . There are those teachers who feel that applying science to an art is quackery, but I believe that our only safeguard against the charlatan is general knowledge of the most accurate information available.
>
> If you are one who has always preferred the empirical approach, perhaps you should read my last chapter first. You may then agree that the knowledge of literal fact is the only justifiable basis for the use of imagery and other indirect methods. Whether you are a singer or a teacher of singing, I hope you will find here truths which you may profitably add to your philosophy, or at least a rationale for harmonizing some of the apparent conflicts in our profession.

These "apparent conflicts" have not disappeared. In 1973, John Carroll Burgin published a study (*Teaching Singing*) of similar approach and structure to that of Fields, in effect bringing Fields' work up to date by analyzing bibliographic data of the period between 1943 and 1971.

In 1978, Brent Jeffrey Monahan identified the need for yet another such study. He acknowledged the work of Fields and Burgin and of Philip A. Duey's systematic analysis of bel canto sources (*Bel Canto in its Golden Age*, 1951). Monahan's research (*The Art of Singing*, 1978) filled in the period from where Duey's work ended and where Fields' began, the period from 1777 to 1927. Like Burgin's book, it followed a similar format to Fields' study. Monahan drew together the earlier research by posing the questions:

> Are traditional concepts retained throughout the years, are they abandoned, or are they interpreted and expanded in the light of modern scientific investigation? When do concepts not mentioned in bel canto writings emerge? Do certain concepts enjoy only fleeting popularity, and is it possible to trace the history of a concept? (p. 4)

Monahan's work is significant in covering the 19th century, a period of change from an emphasis on the empirical methods of the "old Italian school" to a more scientific approach. During this period, Manuel Garcia's scientific investigations of the singing voice formed part of the general climate of scientific investigations in the fields of anatomy, physiology, acoustics, and orthoepy (the science of the pronunciation of words).

Another work that has clarified some of the sources of disagreement and confusion in the teaching of singing is Richard Miller's *English, French, German and Italian Techniques of Singing: A Study in National Tonal Preferences and How They Relate to Functional Efficiency* (1977). Miller identified basic areas of vocal technique where national approaches frequently stand in opposition to each other: breath management, registration, resonance, vowel formation and modification, vocal coloration, "cover," "placement," laryngeal positioning, buccal and pharyngeal postures, the attack, vibrato rate, voice classification, and the uses of falsetto. His investigation attributed many national tendencies in singing to language and "national temperament" factors:

> there are compelling reasons for associating varying national attitudes toward vocalism with overall cultural attitudes ... vocal techniques are but the means for achieving certain sounds which most please a particular cultural unit. Specific kinds of vocal literature and specific kinds of vocal sounds have evolved which directly correspond to national temperaments. (p. 194)

Miller's comparison of the distinctly national techniques led him to conclude that "extremes of nationalism in vocal pedagogy often are based upon the distortion of physical function" (1977, p. 203) and that "a wise singer will look for that internationalization of technique which closely corresponds to the best elements of the historical tradition of the Italian School" (p. 206). It is on this basis that his 1986 book, *The Structure of Singing. System and Art in Vocal Technique*, was predicated. In that book, Miller presented categories of technical problems, exercises to assist in establishing technical skills dependent on optimum physical function, and information on the voice as a physical-acoustic instrument. The introduction articulated, yet again, the problem already outlined by Fields, Burgin, and Monahan:

> any vocal technique involves making assumptions, of varying degrees of specificity as well as of accuracy, concerning the physical production of sound. Differing viewpoints exist with respect not only to aesthetic preference but to the most appropriate physical means for producing the desired sound. (p. xix)

But here a new criterion of judgment was introduced, surely an outcome of late 20th-century scientific certainties about voice:

> The success of any technical approach to singing must be measured by how nearly it arrives at the planned aesthetic result with the least cost.
> Freedom of function in singing ought to count heavily in determining which vocal sounds are most pleasing. The highest possible degree of physical freedom may well be the best indicator of the reliability of aesthetic judgment on the singing voice. (Miller, 1986, pp. xix–xx)

As discussed above, conflicts and confusions between the findings of voice science and the traditional assumptions of vocal pedagogy have been noted by Fields (1947), Vennard (1967), Burgin (1973), Monahan (1978), and Miller (1977, 1986). All these works are concerned with clarifying what physical means are used to achieve aesthetically desirable vocal sound. In addition, Miller's work makes explicit a concern that is implicit in many other writings, that is, that judgment of what is aesthetically desirable needs to be informed by judgment about freedom of physical function. For teachers of singing to make a judgment of what is involved in freedom of physical function, they need to be knowledgeable about voice production.

This book is concerned with the physical bases of voice production—what we know about how the vocal instrument works. The next chapter gives a brief overview of that instrument, while the following chapters assess the scientific literature on breath management, phonation, resonance and articulation, registration and vocal health relevant to the teaching of singing. In the last chapter I return again to vocal pedagogy, relating the specific physical aspects of vocal technique to broader pedagogical concerns.

## References

Atterbury, B. W., & Richardson, C. P. (1995). *The experience of teaching general music.* New York: McGraw-Hill.

Bérard, J.-B. (1969). *L'art du chant* (S. Murray, Trans.). Milwaukee, WI: Pro Musica Press. (Original work published 1755)

Bukofzer, M. F. (1947). *Music in the Baroque era.* New York: Norton.

Burgin, J. (1973). *Teaching singing.* Metuchen, NJ: Scarecrow Press.

Caccini, G. (1970). *Le nuove musiche* (H. Wiley Hitchcock, Ed.). Madison, WI: A-R Editions. (Original work published 1602)

Callaghan, J. (1998). Singing teachers and voice science—An evaluation of voice teaching in Australian tertiary institutions. *Research Studies in Music Education, 10*, 25–41.

Celetti, R. (1991). *A history of bel canto* (F. Fuller, Trans.). Oxford, England: Clarendon Press.

Duey, P. A. (1951). *Bel canto in its golden age. A study of its teaching concepts.* New York: King's Crown Press.

Durrant, C., & Welch, G. (1995). *Making sense of music. Foundations for music education.* London: Cassell.

Fields, V. A. (1947). *Training the singing voice. An analysis of the working concepts contained in recent contributions to vocal pedagogy.* New York: King's Crown Press.

Galliver, D. (1974). Cantare con affetto—Keynote of the bel canto. *Studies in Music, 8*, 1–7.

Garcia, M. (1982). *Hints on singing* (B. Garcia, Trans.) (rev. ed.). New York: Joseph Patelson Music House. (Original work published 1894)

Heriot, A. (1956). *The castrati in opera.* London: Secker & Warburg.

Marchesi, M. (1901). *Ten singing lessons.* New York: Harper & Brothers.

Marchesi, M. (n.d., 19—). *Theoretical and practical vocal method.* London: Enoch.

Mancini, G. (1967). *Practical reflections on figured singing. The editions of 1774 and 1777 compared* (E. Foreman, Ed. & Trans.). Champaign, IL: Pro Musica Press.

Manén, L. (1987). *Bel canto. The teaching of the classical Italian song-schools, its decline and restoration.* Oxford, England: Oxford University Press.

Miller, R. (1977). *English, French, German and Italian techniques of singing: A study in national tonal preferences and how they relate to functional efficiency.* Metuchen, NJ: Scarecrow Press.

Miller, R. (1986). *The structure of singing. System and art in vocal technique.* New York: Schirmer Books.

Miller, R. (1995). The choral conductor as teacher of vocal technique. In: *On the art of singing* (pp. 57–63). New York: Oxford University Press.

Monahan, B. J. (1978). *The art of singing. A compendium of thoughts on singing published between 1777 and 1927.* Metuchen, NJ: Scarecrow Press.

Palisca, C. V. (1968). *Baroque music.* Englewood Cliffs, NJ: Prentice-Hall.

Paschke, D. V. (1975). Translator's Preface to M. Garcia, *A complete treatise on the art of singing: Part two* (pp. ii–xii). New York: Da Capo Press.

Phillips, K. H. (1992). *Teaching kids to sing.* New York: Schirmer Books.

Seiler, E. (1890). *The voice in singing.* Philadelphia: J. B. Lippincott.

Tosi, P.F. (1987). *Observations on the florid song* (Galliard, Trans., M. Pilkington, Ed.). London: Stainer & Bell. (Original work published 1743)

Vennard, W. (1967). *Singing—the mechanism and the technic* (rev. ed.). New York: Carl Fischer.

Weaver, W. (1980). *The golden century of Italian opera from Rossini to Puccini.* London: Thames & Hudson.

# CHAPTER

# 2

# The Voice as a Musical Instrument

*What is now proved was once only imagin'd.*
*—William Blake*

The joint enterprise of the student and teacher is enabling use of the human voice as a musical instrument and aesthetic communicator. That instrument is, of course, the whole person. This is why singing is such a human and moving activity, both for those who do it and for those who listen. In order to help student singers play the vocal instrument to communicate aesthetic meanings, teachers need to know how that instrument works, not just in overview, but in the specifics and their involvement with the larger coordinations. In coming to that understanding, practitioners resort to talking about body and brain, about emotion and vocal apparatus, about music and language, and about perception and cognition. Chapters 3 through 7 discuss voice-science findings about the specifics of the vocal apparatus. The description below of the larger coordinations supplies the context for the understanding of the specifics and their applicability in the teaching of singing.

## The Soma and the Body

The vocal instrument is the body. As Leppert said, "Whatever else music is 'about,' it is *inevitably* about the body; music's aural and visual presence constitutes both a relation to and a representation of the body" (1993, p. xx).

But there are two different and sometimes diametrically opposing ways of observing and understanding the body. One way is from a first-person perspective, from the inside. This body is the soma. For singers, developing a highly-tuned proprioceptive sense—a knowledge of the soma—is essential in using the vocal instrument effectively, both from a physical and an aesthetic point of view. The other way is from a third-person perspective, from the outside. This is the physical body, characterized by universal laws of physics and chemistry. For scientists, collecting data from observation and measurement of human bodies is essential to an understanding of vocal physiology and acoustics.

Failure to distinguish between these different points of view leads to fundamental misunderstandings and hinders both teacher-student communication and interdisciplinary communication. A complete understanding of the vocal instrument requires both an inside and an outside view, and a singing teacher must cultivate both aspects of the art form.

## Hearing, Feeling, and Thinking

The senses are what form the link between the inside and the outside body. It is the human body that sees, hears, feels, perceives, and makes sense of its surroundings. That same body may be thinking language and music while apprehending internal sensations of vibration, movement, and sound, and while attending and responding to external sensations such as the sound of its own voice and the sight and sound of instrumental accompaniment, other singers, and an audience.

The organ essential to this process is the ear, not only in providing auditory input, but in its control of symmetry and balance. The two functions are intimately related, with the auditory system supplying the brain with data on the nature and location of vibrations in the air (perceived as sounds) and the vestibular system of the inner ear providing data on the position of the body. In any type of music making these two functions come together. Anthony Storr even claimed that because music can order our muscular system, "it is also able to order our mental contents. A perceptual system originally designed to inform us of spatial relationships by means of imposing symmetry can be incorporated and transformed into a means of structuring our inner world." (1992, p. 41). Certainly, in singing, auditory, vestibular, and oral functions are coordinated as one in responding to thought, emotion, and sensory feedback. This may account for the association over centuries, in a wide range of cultures, of voicing with meditation and spiritual experience.

The ear forms the link between the vocal apparatus and the brain. Essential to singing is both audition (hearing) and audiation (mental hearing). Audiation also provides the link between music and language and between singing and movement. Audiation is the term used by Edwin Gordon to describe the ability to hear and comprehend musical sound that is no longer present, or that may never have been present: "Audiation is to music what thought is to speech" (1993, p. 13). This ability is essential for all musical thought. Serafine (1988) proposed that a theory of music is at the same time a theory of music cognition and musical thinking. She defined cognition in music, in listening as well as in composing and performing, as "an active, constructive process" (p. 7), dependent on perception, but not the same as perception. Music listening is a unique thinking process where the "art form is not considered a clearly specified external object, but rather an internal, subjective entity springing from mental operations" (p. 233).

While it may be possible to play (badly) a musical instrument without audiation or musical thought, relying purely on mechanical movement, it is not possible to sing without it. Alfred Tomatis' work built on this knowledge that "one sings with one's ear" (1991, p. 44), working on "good auditory receptivity" and "good self-listening" (p. 49). He emphasized that the right ear is dominant in singing, because "in the feedback loop of self-listening, which connects the hearing apparatus to the larynx, the right ear will be closer to the organs of speech than the left" (p. 50).

## Speaking and Singing/Language and Music

The process of hearing, perceiving, and remembering sound forms a loop with the production of sound. In speaking and singing, the sounds being produced by the vocal mechanism are constantly being fed through this loop, dictating what is produced by the vocal apparatus. Even when the physical sound is not there, humans are able to audiate the music we see notated or are about to improvise, just as we are able to hear mentally what we read silently or what we are about to say. Audiation, then, is a process involving physical hearing, perception, cognition, and cultural conditioning.

In recent years, the likelihood of physical and mental links between music and language has been reinforced by investigation into fetal and neonatal development. The fetal sound environment is dominated by the sounds of the mother's body, the sounds of her respiratory and digestive systems and her movements and phonations (Abrams & Gerhardt, 1997). Infants in the womb react both to unstructured noise and to music with movements that their mothers can feel (Storr, 1992). It seems that the origins of both music and language lie in the connection between the neural development of the fetus and this early sound environment. After birth, the affective expressions of crooning, cooing, and babbling develop into speech and song (Storr), with the distinction between speech and song often unclear (Welch, 1994).

Alone among musicians, singers have the joy—and the difficulty—of dealing with words as well as music. Introducing language into the music raises issues related to meaning, phrasing, style, memory, and the need to know several languages. Even more basic, however, is the fact that articulation of words affects the whole instrument: breath management, laryngeal function, and resonance. There is little point in teachers having a good abstract knowledge of vocal anatomy, physiology, and acoustics if they do not have sufficient knowledge of articulatory phonetics to appreciate how the working of the instrument is affected by the demands of different languages.

Then there are the similarities between language and music as semiotic systems using the medium of sound. Specific relationships may exist between music and the meaning of the words, or in the structural relationships between music and text. Under structural relationships between music and linguistic features, two groups may be identified: (i) the relationship between music and linguistic features such as lines, rhyme, and stanza that are present only in poetry, and (ii) the relationship between music and linguistic features found in language at large such as stress, length, tone, and intonation (Nettl, 1964). Full understanding of a song thus rests not only on music or words, but on more general linguistic understandings as well as understanding of the music-language relationship in bodies of vocal music, and in particular compositions.

### The Vocal Instrument

Regarded as a musical instrument, the voice consists of an actuator (the energy produced by the respiratory apparatus), a vibrator (the vocal folds), and a resonator (the vocal tract). This instrument must be capable of producing the requisite pitch, loudness, duration and timbre, and of responding to higher level demands in relation to musical phrasing and articulation of text.

Control over pitch and loudness requires control of the airstream and of the vocal folds. Pitch is the perceptual correlate of phonation frequency—the repetition rate of the glottal pulses—which is mainly determined by the tension and the mass of the vocal folds. Loudness is the perceptual correlate of intensity, which is determined by the amount of excitation that the glottal waves deliver to the air in the vocal tract (Baken, 1991). This depends largely on the interaction between subglottal pressure and the resistance of the vocal folds to the airflow. Resonance factors may also influence the perception of loudness. Control over pitch and loudness together is a feat of fine coordination, because the singer must judge by feel the amount of subglottal pressure and glottal resistance and the appropriate vocal fold adjustment required to sing high soft notes, to sing low loud notes, and to manage crescendo and diminuendo (Callaghan, 1995).

The vocal folds consist of multiple layers, each having different mechanical properties and each subject to different adjustments from the laryngeal muscles. Hirano (1988) contrasted this structure with the structure of the strings of many musical instruments and of the vocal folds of other animals, pointing out that the human structure is particularly well adapted to singing. The complex adjustments possible within each layer and between layers mean that the voice is capable of finer tuning than is possible on string instruments.

The ability to sing the required relative durations (rhythm) requires coordination of the whole singing instrument in response to a clear mental concept of the musical demands. This coordination depends largely on breath management, the ability to inhale in the time available and to manage the flow of breath to meet the demands of music in relation to length of phrase, leaps, and dynamics (Callaghan, 1995).

The timbre of the voice is determined by the functioning of the vocal folds in the production of the voice source and the acoustic filtering of this sound through the configuration of the vocal tract. The shape of the glottal pulses determines the potential quality of the note sung. The glottal wave may be smoothly varying (rounded) and contain little energy at the higher overtones; or it may have a sharp "corner," (changing in slope) and contain relatively more energy at the higher overtones (Rothenberg, 1984).

Turbulence and perturbation are also part of the voice source. Some turbulence is perceived as a softness, or velvety quality, in the sound. More turbulence might be heard as breathiness, or perhaps huskiness, and too much turbulence contributes to the perception of hoarseness (Baken, 1991). Female voices have a longer open phase and a posterior opening, creating aspiration noise in the region of the third formant, which is perceived as a breathier quality than that of male voices (Mendoza, Valencia, Muñoz, & Trujillo, 1996).

The voice source produced by the vibrating vocal folds is a spectrum of tones, comprising the fundamental (the lowest frequency or pitch of the note) and the overtones or harmonics at integer multiples of the fundamental. The air in the vocal tract acts as a resonator, selecting out frequencies from the sound source according to the configuration of the tract. Frequencies that fit the resonator optimally are formant frequencies, and it is the partials closest to these formant frequencies that are transmitted with increased amplitude (Sundberg, 1987).

The timbre of a note, both in regard to vowel quality and voice color, depends on the formant frequencies. A movement in any of the articulators generally affects the frequencies of all formants. The two lowest formants determine vowel quality, while the third, fourth, and fifth are responsible for personal voice characteristics such as voice type and timbre (Sundberg, 1991). Timbre is linked to perception of pitch through the distribution of formant frequencies characteristic of particular vowels: for example, a pitch sung on /i/, with its high second formant, may be perceived as higher than the same pitch sung on /u/, with its relatively low second formant.

The length and shape of the tract are changed by the position; of the larynx; the shape of the pharynx; the position of the tongue, soft palate, and mandible; and the shape of the lips. The articulators are interrelated, allowing subtle adjustments to vocal timbre. Minor alterations in the configuration of these structures may produce substantial changes in voice quality. These structures are also used for the articulation of words. Therefore, in singing, vocal timbre and production of text are intimately linked. The articulation of continuous text set to music affects the whole instrument: breath management, laryngeal function, and resonance.

Because the singer is the musical instrument, the teaching of vocal technique usually concerns the use of body and mind in achieving particular musical ends. Posture, breath management, the attack or onset, resonance, aesthetically pleasing tone, word articulation, unifying vocal registers, and extending range (e.g., Husler & Rodd-Marling, 1976; Miller, 1986, 1993; Doscher, 1994; Bunch, 1995; David, 1995) and issues of health and overall body use (e.g., Proctor, 1980; McKinney, 1982; Miller, 1986; Sataloff, 1991; Titze, 1994; Bunch, 1995) all affect the instrument.

To facilitate the best use of the body as a singing instrument, the teacher needs an understanding of vocal anatomy, physiology, and acoustics. Vennard pointed out that:

> A teacher should know what he is talking about, but that does not mean that he gives a voice lesson as if he were teaching anatomy. All muscles are controlled indirectly, in terms of their effects beyond themselves. (1967, p. 19)

Nevertheless, such an understanding facilitates efficient teaching of the physical skills of singing, provides the basis of diagnosis of vocal faults, and ensures that technical work is informed by principles of vocal health. Information on vocal anatomy is now easily accessible to singing teachers, not only in scientific texts but in many pedagogy texts (e.g., Husler & Rodd-Marling, 1976; Miller, 1986; Manén, 1987; Doscher, 1994; Bunch, 1995; David, 1995). This book is therefore concerned more with recent studies in vocal physiology and acoustics as they relate to singing.

## Control of the Vocal Instrument

Information is extracted from a vocal utterance by recognition of patterns in the sequence of sounds, the patterns being identified by their boundaries, and by discontinuity in relation to continuity. In an article on the perceptual aspects of singing, Sundberg stated that "the singer must gain control over all perceptually relevant voice parameters, so that they do not change by accident and signal an unintended boundary" (1994, p. 120). Technical control of all vocal parameters is therefore a prerequisite for artistic expression.

This overall control of the instrument is of overriding concern in the teaching of vocal technique. While this concern motivates most writing on singing technique, only a small proportion of the literature

explicitly addresses matters of overall coordination (e.g., Miller, 1986; Doscher, 1994; Bunch, 1995). Doscher, whose book is titled *The Functional Unity of the Singing Voice*, wrote of the "sensuous building blocks" of the art that work as a functional unit (p. 167).

While practitioners most often consider posture in relation to respiration, the posturing of the body contributes not only to controlled respiration, but to all aspects of sound production, through the relationships established between the respiratory system, the phonatory mechanism, and the resonators, and through feedback from the muscles to the nervous system. Singers may also call on postural muscles to play an active role in stabilizing the body under considerable stress when producing loud, sustained vocalization over a wide pitch range. Doscher's reference to posture as "a kinesthetic barometer for the entire body, continually giving us conceptual data on body position, muscle tone, energy potential, and balance" (1994, p. 69) is apt.

While singing teachers devote much time to skills related to resonance, many teachers see conscious control of the larynx as either impossible or undesirable; they assert that in "good" singing, the performer is unaware of any laryngeal sensation. Yet exercises concerned with the onset of phonation and register-blending primarily involve laryngeal control. Singers also experience the varying laryngeal loading of different vowels and the effect of palatal elevation on laryngeal functioning. There seems to be no reason why the fine laryngeal control used intuitively in many physiological functions such as laughing, crying, and sighing should not be brought under conscious control for singing. With these affective expressions, it is possible to achieve an instinctive balance between breath management, adjustment of the articulators, and laryngeal action.

Theories of tone placement attempt to correlate breath management, resonance balance, and the singer's physical sensations. Differences in timbre have corresponding locations of resonance sensation. Titze (1981) suggested that the singer's sensation of where tone is localized may be related to the localization of pressure maxima in the vocal tract and thus "singing in the mask" or "resonating the cheek bones" or "aiming the tone toward the hard palate just behind the upper incisors" may all be related to achieving an acoustic pressure maximum at a specified location in the vocal tract.

The singer's sensations of resonance may, however, be unreliable as an indicator of timbre, or may differ from the teacher's. In adhering rigidly to one theory of placement for all voice types, there is also the danger of creating uneven timbre across the range and accentuating register problems, since the success of increasing acoustic output with formant tuning varies with fundamental frequency. Again, the danger is that such an approach may become fixed, and freedom of adjustment in response to aural cues may be diminished.

All vocal functions are controlled neurologically: The laryngeal muscles position the larynx and achieve adduction of the vocal folds; the diaphragm and intercostal muscles raise subglottic pressure; the muscles of articulation adjust the length and shape of the vocal tract; and the middle ear muscles reduce the sensitivity of the ear just before the initiation of phonation—all in response to a neurological signal (Sataloff, 1992). Recent investigations into the role played in voicing by the periaqueductal gray matter of the midbrain have suggested that the re-creation of emotional experience in performance may allow access to subtleties of respiratory and laryngeal muscle patterning and particular vocal qualities integrated in that area of the brain (Larson, 1988; Davis, Zhang, Winkworth, & Bandler, 1996).

Essential to vocal control is feedback. For singers, feedback may come from external sources or from internal sensory sources (Titze, 1982). External sources include the human response of audience, teachers, or colleagues. Internal feedback—visual, tactile, auditory, kinesthetic, and proprioceptive—is usually immediate and directly related to what goes on in the body. The effect of visual feedback from instrumentation on learning breath management and resonance control strategies is becoming more important. The mirror, the simplest form of visual feedback, has been in use in the singing studio for centuries. Recently computer-assisted visual feedback has become available.

Tactile, kinesthetic, and proprioceptive feedback is supplied through sensory receptors located throughout the entire body. Tongue position, jaw position, and tongue contact with the lips, teeth, or palate are monitored continuously during singing (Titze, 1982) and, as previously mentioned, the posture of the body provides proprioceptive feedback that is important in phonation.

Auditory feedback, transmitted from the ear through the brain stem to the cerebral cortex, is also used as a control by the singer. It allows the singer to match the sound produced with the sound intended (Sataloff, 1992; Titze, 1994). Tactile feedback from the throat and muscles also may help with the fine-tuning of vocal output (Sataloff, 1992).

For singers, sensations of vibration constitute a major source of control. Books on voice production for singers and teachers commonly have referred to location of vibration sensations (e.g., Husler & Rodd-Marling, 1976; Proctor, 1980; Miller, 1986), particularly in relation to airflow and resonance. Schutte and Miller (1984) pointed out that these sensations differ from or exceed the vibratory sensations of speech.

Several studies have clarified the source and location of sensations experienced by singers. Sundberg (1990), for example, found that the voice source, particularly the amplitude of its fundamental, was reflected in chest wall vibrations, particularly at the center of the sternum. Even when the overall sound pressure level remained essentially constant, changing the mode of phonation from pressed to flow increased chest vibrations. This change led to changes in the amplitude of sternum vibrations, providing tactile feedback for phonation at low fundamental frequencies (up to 300 Hz). This would serve as a useful nonauditory (room-independent) signal for voluntary control.

Titze (1994) relates the singer's sensation of where the vowel is localized (focused) to the localization of pressure maxima of the standing waves of the vocal tract. Different vowels have high pressures in different regions, the /i/ vowel having pressures high in the palatal region, the /u/ vowel having pressures high in the velar region, and the /ɑ/ vowel having pressures high in the pharynx. The singer may use these sensations in modifying vowels as needed.

A study by Estill, Baer, Honda, and Harris (1984) found support for the common assumption that the palate is active in the production of high frequencies and differentially active depending on the voice quality. The researchers recorded the activity of the levator palatini, palatopharyngeus, the middle constrictor, and the geniohyoid muscles while a singer produced six vocal qualities over a two-octave range. Electromyographic recordings showed, in all six qualities, an increase in muscle activity with increase in fundamental frequency. Since these muscles are located in the center of the head, their contraction may contribute to the feelings experienced by many singers

that the palate is active in the upper part of the range, or in high intensity tones at any frequency.

Vocal control, then, depends on a complex of fine motor coordinations directed by neurological signals and monitored by a range of external and internal feedback.

## The Physiologically Gifted Voice

From time to time, someone advances the theory that premier singers must be physiologically gifted. In societies where singing has become quite divorced from speaking, where the general populace does not sing (except perhaps at the football stadium) and where the singing of "high art" music and "popular" music have become very different, it is commonly believed that elite singers must be physiologically gifted. Researchers, however, have yet to prove this point.

Ingo Titze (1998) relied on theoretical models of voice and physical laws to suggest five attributes of a physiologically gifted voice: a wide cricothyroid space; strong cricothyroid and thyroarytenoid muscles; a thick mucosa with an optimal fiber-liquid concentration; symmetry between the left and right vocal folds; and the ability to activate adjacent muscles selectively. This cluster of physical attributes is analogous to those that may be identified as physical predispositions for playing other instruments (e.g., lip and jaw attributes in brass playing) and can contribute to a fine voice. A wide cricothyroid space makes a wide pitch range more likely. Strong cricothyroid and thyroartytenoid muscles allow efficient length and tension changes in the vocal folds. The quality of the mucosa affects the ability to create the optimal mucosal wave. Symmetry between the left and right vocal folds (and across the entire larynx) contributes to normal vocal fold vibration and good control of pitch, loudness, and onset. The ability to activate adjacent muscles selectively is one required for all skilled physical activity.

In a 1991 article, however, Thomas Cleveland recounted his investigation into the laryngeal characteristics of some premier singers. He used nasal endoscopy to examine the larynges of a number of premier singers and videotaped the examinations. He was disappointed to discover that these premier singers did not have the "class" larynges he expected; they exhibited the range of difference and asymmetries common across the population. He concluded that each larynx "is an original, and its potential lies far beyond its appearance" (p. 51).

While certain physical characteristics may amount to a predisposition for singing, learned skills are more important. In reviewing the differences between breathing, phonation, and articulation patterns in speech and singing, Johan Sundberg (1990) identified reasons why singers are "special"; these relate largely to the ability to meet the heightened demands of pitch, duration, dynamics, and timbre made by many musical genres. The nature and applications of these physical skills will be considered in greater detail in following chapters.

## To See What One Thinks, Hears, and Feels

Since the 1960s, there have been major developments in voice science. In singing, technical matters pose unique problems in that the singer's instrument is the body. The component parts of the singer's instrument consist of many different body parts that are used for other activities and require fine coordination to achieve expressive singing. Any part, or the overall coordination of all parts, of the instrument is susceptible to the singer's general physical, intellectual, and emotional state. Until recently, many of the working parts of this instrument could not be viewed in operation.

Sophisticated instrumentation now makes possible real-time visual and aural feedback on the acoustic effects of particular vocal maneuvers. Through the use of videoendoscopy, for example, it is possible for a singer to see on a video screen the operation of the larynx as the sound is being produced; other computer analyzers give a visual display of the acoustic properties of the sound as it is made. Such equipment makes it possible to diagnose vocal problems, to teach more efficiently, and to match specific prescriptions for vocal effort with the acoustic effects they produce.

Since about 1970, many scientific studies of voice have been carried out using technology to view the larynx in operation, measure muscular effort, determine subglottal pressure, and record the acoustic nature of vocal sound. In the last 15 years it has become more common for writings on singing pedagogy to refer to scientific findings, and for scientific writings to comment on the implications for pedagogy. For these reasons, the following chapters refer mainly to the literature of the last 30 years.

## References

Abrams, R. M., & Gerhardt, K. K. (1997). Some aspects of the foetal sound environment. In I. Deliege & J. Sloboda (Eds.), *Perception and cognition of music*. Hove, England: Psychology Press.

Baken, R. J. (1991). An overview of laryngeal function for voice production. In R. T. Sataloff (Ed.), *Professional voice: The science and art of clinical care* (pp. 19–47). New York: Raven Press.

Bunch, M. (1995). *Dynamics of the singing voice* (3rd ed.). Wien: Springer-Verlag.

Callaghan, J. (1995). Fundamental teaching units of vocal pedagogy: Paper 1. *Australian Voice, 1,* 1–5.

Cleveland, T. (1991). Vocal pedagogy in the twenty-first century: Does the "premier" singer's larynx show visible differences from the normal singer's larynx? *The NATS Journal, 47*(4), 50–51.

David, M. (1995). *The new voice pedagogy*. Lanham, MD: Scarecrow Press.

Davis, P. J., Zhang, S. P., Winkworth, A., & Bandler, R. (1996). Neural control of vocalization: Respiratory and emotional influences. *Journal of Voice, 10*(1), 23–38.

Doscher, B. (1994). *The functional unity of the singing voice* (2nd ed.). Metuchen, NJ: Scarecrow Press.

Estill, J., Baer, T., Honda, K., & Harris, K. S. (1984). The control of pitch and quality, Part I: An EMG study of supralaryngeal activity in six voice qualities. In V. L. Lawrence (Ed.), *Transcripts of the twelfth symposium, Care of the professional voice, 1983, Pt I* (pp. 86–91). New York: The Voice Foundation.

Gordon, E. E. (1993). *Learning sequences in music. Skill, content, and patterns. A music learning theory*. Chicago: GIA Publications.

Hirano, M. (1988). The G. Paul Moore Lecture. Vocal mechanisms in singing: Laryngological and phoniatric aspects. *Journal of Voice, 1*(1), 51–69.

Husler, F., & Rodd-Marling, Y. (1976). *Singing. The physical nature of the vocal organ*. London: Hutchinson.

Larson, C. R. (1988). Brain mechanisms involved in the control of vocalization. *Journal of Voice, 2*(4), 301–311.

Leppert, R. (1993). *The sight of sound. Music, representation, and the history of the body.* Berkeley, CA: University of California Press.

McKinney, J. C. (1982). *The diagnosis & correction of vocal faults.* Nashville, TN: Broadman Press.

Manén, L. (1987). *Bel canto. The teaching of the classical Italian song-schools, its decline and restoration.* Oxford, England: Oxford University Press.

Mendoza, E., Valencia, N., Muñoz, J., & Trujillo, H. (1996). Differences in voice quality between men and women: Use of the long-term average spectrum (LTAS). *Journal of Voice, 10*(1), 59–66.

Miller, R. (1986). *The structure of singing. System and art in vocal technique.* New York: Schirmer Books.

Miller, R. (1993). *Training tenor voices.* New York: Schirmer Books.

Nettl, B. (1964). *Theory and method in ethnomusicology.* London: Free Press.

Proctor, D. F. (1980). *Breathing, speech, and song.* Wien: Springer-Verlag.

Rothenberg, M. (1984). Source-tract acoustic interaction and voice quality. In V. L. Lawrence (Ed.), *Transcripts of the twelfth symposium, Care of the professional voice, 1983 (Pt I,* pp. 25–31). New York: The Voice Foundation.

Sataloff, R. T. (1991). Clinical anatomy and physiology of the voice. In R. T. Sataloff (Ed.), *Professional voice. The science and art of clinical care.* New York: Raven Press.

Sataloff, R. T. (1992). The human voice. *Scientific American 267*(6), 108–115.

Schutte, H. K., & Miller, R. (1984). Resonance balance in register categories of the singing voice: A spectral analysis study. *Folia phoniatrica, 36,* 289–295.

Serafine, M. L. (1988). *Music as cognition. The development of thought in sound.* New York: Columbia University Press.

Storr, A. (1992). *Music and the mind.* London: Harper Collins.

Sundberg, J. (1987). *The science of singing.* Dekalb, IL: Northern Illinois University Press.

Sundberg, J. (1990). Chest wall vibrations in singers. *Journal of Research in Singing and Applied Vocal Pedagogy, XIII*(2), 25–53.

Sundberg, J. (1991). Vocal tract resonance. In Sataloff R. T. (Ed.), *Professional voice. The science and art of clinical care* (pp. 49–68). New York: Raven Press.

Sundberg, J. (1994). Perceptual aspects of singing. *Journal of Voice, 8*(2), 106–122.

Titze, I. R. (1981). Is there a scientific explanation for tone focus and voice placement? *The NATS Bulletin, 7*(5), 26–27.

Titze, I. R. (1982). Sensory feedback in voice production. *The NATS Bulletin, 38*(4), 32.

Titze, I. R. (1994). *Principles of voice production.* Englewood Cliffs, NJ: Prentice Hall.

Titze, I. R. (1998). Voice research: Five ingredients of a physiologically gifted voice. *Journal of Singing, 54*(3), 45–46.

Tomatis, A. A. (1991). *The conscious ear. My life of transformation through listening* (S. Lushington, Trans., B. M. Thompson, Ed.). New York: Station Hill Press.

Vennard, W. (1967). *Singing—the mechanism and the technic* (rev. ed.). New York: Carl Fischer.

Welch, G. F. (1994). The assessment of singing. *Psychology of Music, 22*, 3–19.

# C H A P T E R

# 3

# *Breath Management*

**W**riters on singing emphasize that efficient breath management is fundamental to vocal control in expressive singing. As Miller put it, "any error in vocal technique, or any accomplishment of technical skill in singing, usually can be traced to techniques of breath management; control of the breath is synonymous with control of the singing instrument" (1986, p. 37).

Singers need to control respiration in order to meet musical demands in relation to phrase length, pitch range, loudness, musical articulation, time between phrases, and so on. In addition, breath management must be geared to producing the vocal quality appropriate to the particular style. In most cases, classical singers initiate phrases at approximately 70% of vital capacity and use breath that is beyond the resting expiratory level. Cleveland (1998) compared this breath management strategy with that of country singers, who, while they also use breath beyond the resting expiratory level, initiate phrases at about 55% of vital capacity, a point close to tidal breathing. Country singers use similar breath strategies for speech and singing, and therefore their singing sounds more like speech, which is stylistically appropriate.

According to Hixon and Hoffman (1979, p. 9) breathing for (classical) singing differs from resting breathing in that it uses:

- a far greater range of lung volumes
- higher expiratory alveolar pressures and lower inspiratory alveolar pressures
- lower expiratory airflow and higher inspiratory airflow

- longer expiratory breathing phases and shorter inspiratory breathing phases
- torso shapes that depart more from the relaxed configuration of the chest wall

For classical singers, the transition from inspiration to expiration is characterized by equal and opposite decreases in abdomen volume, increases in rib cage volume occurring without a change in lung volume, and the transition from expiration to inspiration by rapid decrements in lung volume immediately preceding the onset of inspiration (Cleveland, 1998).

Many researchers (e.g., Allen & Wilder, 1977; McGlone, 1977; Brown, Rothman, & Williams, 1978; Watson & Hixon, 1985; Sundberg, 1987; Brown, Hunt, & Williams, 1988; Hoit, Christie, Watson, & Cleveland, 1996; Cleveland, 1998) have noted that accomplished trained singers use respiratory strategies different from both those of untrained singers and those that they themselves use in normal speech. Some researchers (e.g., Brown et al., 1988; Sundberg, Iwarsson, & Billström, 1995) have suggested that accomplished singers may have superior sensory abilities that help them develop finely tuned control of subglottal pressure and airflow to meet musical demands. The research into respiration in singing suggests that it is training, rather than any particular physiological endowment, that produces this control. An understanding of respiration and of the factors involved in breath management is therefore essential for the efficient teaching of singing.

### The Role of the Diaphragm

Reporting a study of different national approaches to singing technique, Miller asserted that "national schools of singing clearly indicate a lack of agreement as to how to approach breath management" (1977, p. 20). He attributed this lack of agreement to differing assumptions about the kinds of muscular action that are thought to occur during the breath cycle, particularly in relation to the control of the musculature that regulates or influences the diaphragm: "Some teachers of singing claim that the diaphragm is an involuntary muscle which can be only indirectly controlled by the action of other controllable muscles; others attempt localized control over its movement" (p. 20).

A 1985 study by Watson and Hixon and a 1987 study by Leanderson, Sundberg, and von Euler (Leanderson et al., 1987a) reached contradictory conclusions about the role of the diaphragm in breath management for singing. The Watson and Hixon study recorded anteroposterior diameter changes of the rib cage and abdomen in six baritones during four respiratory, four speaking, and four singing activities. The respiratory activities were vital-capacity maneuvers, muscular relaxations of the respiratory apparatus at different lung volumes, and isovolume shape changes of the respiratory apparatus at a single lung volume. The speaking activities were two minutes of spontaneous conversation, reading aloud a declarative passage, reading the same passage at what the singer judged to be twice his normal volume, and reading aloud the words of the first verse of *The Star Spangled Banner*. The participants sang *The Star Spangled Banner*, two Italian songs, and an aria of the participant's choice, material that required contrasting musical and language demands. Data were collected to calculate lung volume, volume displacements of the rib cage and abdomen, and to infer muscular mechanisms.

The singing training of the participants varied from 5 to 20 years of classical training, their performance experience ranged from largely university or college performances in oratorio and recital to professional opera performance, and their ages ranged from 23 to 38. The researchers made measurements using a noninvasive kinematic procedure requiring little experimental sophistication on the part of the singers and allowing the experimental setup to resemble performance conditions. They described the kinematic procedure as treating the chest wall as a two-part system consisting of the rib cage and abdomen. Relying on the fact that each part displaces volume as it moves (and that together they displace a volume equal to that displaced by the lungs), the procedure enables calculation of the relative volumes displaced by measuring changes in anteroposterior diameter for each part.

These investigators found two principal patterns of inspiration. In one, the volume contribution of the rib cage exceeded that of the abdomen. In the other, the contribution of the abdomen exceeded that of the rib cage during the first part of inspiration, followed by equal rib cage and abdominal displacement, then followed by a predominant rib cage contribution at the end of inspiration. They also found two patterns for the expiratory part of the breath cycle. In one, the volume contribution of the rib cage was greater. In the other, the abdominal contribution was greater for the first part of expiration, followed by equal rib cage and abdominal displacement, and then by predominant rib cage contribution during the last part of expiration. There were also two main types of transition from expiration to inspiration, one in which rib cage displacements predominated and one in which abdominal displacements predominated. Marked changes in relative contributions were associated with musical demands; inward abdominal displacement and outward rib cage displacement were associated with increases in loudness, stress, or high notes, while inward rib cage displacement and outward abdominal displacement were associated with passages involving high flow, as in the case of voiceless fricatives.

Watson and Hixon stated:

> the chest wall was continuously distorted from its relaxed configurations during singing . . . meaning that muscular forces were continuously in operation. The rib cage was found always to be maintained in a more expanded state and the abdomen always to be maintained in a less expanded state than were these two when relaxed at corresponding lung volumes. (1985, p. 116)

They went on to suggest a specific role for the abdomen:

> mainly one of posturing the chest wall in a manner that aids both the rib cage and diaphragm in their primary functions. This role involves the configuration of the chest wall and extends across both phases of the respiratory cycle for singing. (p. 119)

They attributed to the rib cage the major role of pressurization of the pulmonary system in expiration and to the diaphragm the role of inflating the pulmonary system quickly in inspiration.

Taken together, these confusing statements presumably mean that a body posture departing from the usual relaxed state is assumed for classical singing and that the muscles of rib cage and abdomen are active throughout the respiratory cycle. It is not clear exactly what this body posture is, whether it was the same for all six baritones, whether posture related to the different inspiratory patterns observed, and what bearing it had on the finding that all participants used a "belly in" strategy. The authors also acknowledged the difficulty, common to many studies of the singing voice, of assessing the contribution of singing training to the differences in data obtained from the singers used in their study.

The attribution to the abdomen of a posturing role seems at odds with the finding of marked abdominal displacement (presumably produced by muscle activity) accompanying increases in loudness, stress, or high notes. Watson and Hixon's assumption that the diaphragm is active during inspiration but plays no role in controlled expiration is common to many recent writings on singing. Doscher, for example, stated:

Contrary to popular belief, we have little or no voluntary control
over diaphragmatic action. The diaphragm has no proprioceptive
(stimuli arising within an organism) nerve endings, and therefore it
is impossible to experience any sensation of its position or movement. (1994, p. 18)

Control, however, does not only depend on feedback of muscle
length or tension, and there are other sources of feedback—for example, the volume receptors in the lungs themselves.

The assumption made in many singing texts that the diaphragm
is active only during inspiration has been called into question by a
series of experiments conducted by Leanderson and collaborators on
the role of the diaphragm in establishing adequate subglottal pressure
in singing (1984, 1987a, 1987b). In one study (Leanderson, Sundberg,
& von Euler, 1987a), the researchers conducted two different experiments. The first experiment investigated diaphragmatic activity during singing tasks requiring rapid changes in subglottal pressure. Four
trained singers (one tenor and three baritones) performed tasks
demanding rapid changes of subglottal pressure. On the basis that
diaphragmatic activity acts to decrease intrathoracic pressure at the
same time as it exerts positive pressure on the abdominal contents,
pressure above and below the diaphragm was measured to indicate
diaphragmatic activity. This required participants to swallow an
esophageal catheter with two small pressure transducers. Oral pressure during /p/ occlusion was regarded as a good approximation of
subglottal pressure with zero airflow and was measured by a thin
catheter in the corner of the mouth. It is not clear whether this rather
intrusive procedure affected the singing of the participants. Participants used varying strategies in producing the syllable sequence
/pa:pa:pa:.../, in singing octave leaps, and in performing subito forte-
piano tasks; yet all used a similar strategy for performing a trillo and
in singing a coloratura passage. However, individual participants
used similar strategies to perform some tasks and different strategies
to perform others. What the significance of these variations might be
is difficult to assess. Despite the variations, evidence for a consistent
use of the diaphragm was found in all participants.

In this study, the limited number of participants, the fact that
they were all men, and that even among four participants there was
interparticipant variability makes it difficult to assess the application
of these results. From the practitioner point of view, it would be useful to know whether—and, if so, how—the different strategies used
by the singers affected the sound quality they produced. Regardless
of the variations, it was clear that some singers did activate the
diaphragm when there was a need for a rapid decrease of subglottal

pressure, such as when singing a falling octave interval, when shifting from a loud to a soft note, to save air during a /p/ explosion, or in performing a trillo involving a repeated switch between glottal adduction and abduction.

The second experiment in the Leanderson et al. (1987a) study investigated the effect of diaphragmatic activity on the voice source. Two female and four male untrained participants and two trained singers were asked to perform tasks first with an active diaphragm and then with a passive diaphragm. The tasks for the trained and untrained participants were different: The singers sang triads, octaves, and sustained tones of different intensity; the untrained participants sang gliding and sustained tones. The method of measurement was the same as in the first experiment, with sound pressure level measured in addition. The transdiaphragmatic pressure was displayed on an oscilloscope screen as a visual feedback. In some participants, diaphragmatic activity apparently affected vocal fold adduction, producing airflow in the direction of flow phonation (a high amplitude of the flow glottogram combined with a marked closed phase). Again, there was interparticipant variation.

## Body Posture and Breath Management

Breath management involves gravity, elastic recoil, and muscular activity. Clearly, body posture affects all these factors: The downward pull of gravity depends on the posture of the singer; the posture of the torso and the alignment of the spine can affect elastic recoil; the degree of muscular effort and the direction of that effort may be directly influenced by body posture or indirectly by gravity and elastic recoil factors (Cleveland, 1998).

Some singing pedagogies attempt to correct the natural curvature of the spine, mistakenly believing that a perpendicular spine will assist breath management. Attempting to remove the natural curvature of the spine in fact results in misalignment and rigidity, interfering with breath management. Richard Miller recommended adopting the "Garcia position," "that is, placing the back of the hands together dorsally at the sacroiliac region," a maneuver that "assures the natural curvature of the spine, elevates the thoracic cage, and balances the stance" (1999, p. 45).

As is clear from the earlier discussion, the same subglottal pressure can be generated in different ways. For instance, the abdominal wall may be bulging out or pulled in during phonation, depending on the relative activation of the thoracic and abdominal wall musculature. A bulging out of the abdominal wall would also arise as a consequence of diaphragmatic activation (Leanderson & Sundberg, 1988). A number of researchers (e.g., Hixon & Hoffman, 1979; Miller, 1986; Leanderson & Sundberg, 1988; Carroll & Sataloff, 1991; Sataloff, 1992; Sundberg, 1993; Titze, 1994) have discussed the relative merits of the "belly-in" and "belly-out" methods of support. It is not yet clear how these different approaches may affect airflow and other aspects of laryngeal control.

Titze (1994) characterized these two extremes of body posture that position the chest in relation to the abdomen as the "pear-shape-up" approach ("belly-in" method) and the "pear-shape-down" approach ("belly-out" method), or the "up-and-in" and "down-and-out" methods of support. In the "belly-in" approach, the singer places emphasis on keeping the rib cage high and stable; in the "belly-out" approach, the singer places emphasis on maintaining stable abdominal pressure. While Miller (1977) identified many variations in approach to breath management among national schools of singing pedagogy, it is broadly true to say that the German school favors Titze's "pear-shape-down" approach, while the English, French, and Italian schools favor the "pear-shape-up" approach.

In 1979, Hixon and Hoffman analyzed the advantages and disadvantages of these diametrically opposed torso shapes and found that neither was clearly superior to the other. In the "belly-in"

BELLY IN       V.       BELLY OUT

method, both the rib cage expiratory muscles and the diaphragm are at near optimum position on their length-tension characteristics, which means that they are capable of producing rapid, forceful expiratory efforts. The disadvantage of this approach is that abdominal wall muscle activity tends to distend the diaphragm so that it comes under progressively greater passive tension in the inspiratory direction on the rib cage wall, which is counterproductive to the overall expiratory task required for singing. This does not happen in the "belly-out" method, which still has the same rib cage wall advantage as the "belly-in" configuration. An additional advantage of the abdomen-out configuration is that the abdominal wall musculature is placed at near optimum positions on its length-tension characteristic, which means that it is more capable of producing forceful efforts. However, a major disadvantage of this configuration is that the relatively flat diaphragm is in an unfavorable position to generate inspiratory force, which is a limitation when the music demands quick inspiration. Titze (1994) reserved judgment on the relative merits of the different methods, pointing out that Hoit and Hixon's 1986 study suggested body type may be a factor in determining the optimal approach for different individuals.

In their 1985 study (discussed above), Watson and Hixon found that regardless of the beliefs held by participants about their breath management strategy, they all employed "the so-called 'belly in' strategy for singing." They concluded that "unanimous use of this strategy by the participant group suggests that it may have a collection of advantages for the singer toward which he naturally migrates with performance experience" (p. 120). In view of the small number of participants (six) studied and the fact that all participants were of the same voice type and therefore likely to be of the same body type, these results cannot be regarded as generally conclusive for all singers.

In other experiments Leanderson, Sundberg, and von Euler (Leanderson et al., 1987a; Sundberg, Leanderson, & von Euler, 1989) found that when participants used a "belly-out" strategy in conjunction with contracting the diaphragm relatively forcefully throughout the phrase, the trachea exerted an increased pull on the larynx. This tracheal pull increased the need for cricothyroid contraction—that is, the breathing strategy affected the voice control mechanism. Tracheal pull also appeared to reduce glottal adduction, increasing the amplitude of the lowest partial of the voice spectrum. Such a strategy may not be effective for singing at very high pitches, where some larynx elevation is necessary. This may be another area where male-female differences need to be clarified for the purposes of pedagogy.

### *Appoggio* **Technique**

In his 1986 book, *The Structure of Singing*, Miller commented that "widely disseminated techniques of singing have been based on assumed muscle relationships that are patently absurd" and, on the basis of functional efficiency, advocated the *appoggio* technique of the historic Italian school, "a system for combining and balancing muscles and organs of the trunk and neck, controlling their relationships to the supraglottal resonators, so that no exaggerated function of any one of them upsets the whole" (p. 24). In *appoggio* technique

> the sternum must initially find a moderately high position; this position is then retained throughout the inspiration-expiration cycle. . . . Both the epigastric and umbilical regions should be stabilized so that a feeling of internal-external muscular balance is present. This sensation directly influences the diaphragm. . . . Although the lower abdomen (hypogastric, or pubic, region) does not distend, there is a feeling of muscular connection from sternum to pelvis. . . . However, to move out the lower abdomen either during inspiration or during the execution of a phrase, as some singers are taught to do, is foreign to *appoggio* technique. Equally alien is the practice of pulling inward on the pubic area as a means of "supporting" the voice. (p. 24)

While this approach fits Titze's (1994) "pear-shape-up" posture, its emphasis on flexibility seems not to fit either the "belly-out" or "belly-in" methods of support as advocated by many practitioners. Indeed, Miller preferred the term "breath management" to "support." The flexible approach of *appoggio* seems to answer the need for dynamic breath management strategies to meet different musical demands and to suit different body types.

### **The Concept of Support**

Singers and teachers of singing often use the term "support" to refer to the coordinations required to control the interrelated parameters of subglottal pressure and airflow and implying aspects of posture. McKinney defined support as "the dynamic relationship between the breathing-in muscles and the breathing-out muscles whose purpose is to supply adequate breath pressure to the vocal cords for the sustaining of any desired pitch or dynamic level" (1982, pp. 55–56). Thus, breath management for singing also implies control of laryngeal function. What is involved in this, and how the appropriate coordinations can best be taught, are matters of some contention.

In recent years some experimental research has been directed to clarifying what support means in physical terms. A preliminary study by Griffin, Woo, Colton, Casper, and Brewer (1995) aimed to develop an objective definition of the supported singing voice based on physiological characteristics. Other studies relating to subglottal pressure, airflow, and the role of the diaphragm in singing are also relevant to pedagogical approaches to support. Some of these studies are discussed below. Unfortunately, the range of methods used from one study to another, the small number of participants used, and the range of training and performance experience of participants from one study to another—and in some cases within the one study—make evaluation of the experimental evidence and its application to pedagogy difficult.

In the Griffin et al. (1995) study, the participants were eight classically trained singers—four male and four female—having a minimum of a bachelor's degree in vocal performance or five years of private voice study and at least five years of professional solo singing experience in opera, oratorio, or both. They wrote definitions of supported singing voice and descriptions of how it is produced, as well as singing samples of the sustained vowel /ɛ/ (at low, medium, and high pitches defined for each voice) and repetitions of the syllable /bɛp/. Participants defined the supported singing voice as being characterized by resonance, clarity, and extended vocal range produced by correct adjustment of the breathing muscles. The researchers found "supported voice" to be louder and to be more efficient in terms of having increased peak flow and a longer glottal closed phase.

This preliminary study found that breathing patterns were highly variable among participants, but no significant differences in breathing activity were found when the participants produced supported, as opposed to unsupported, voice. It is not stated whether breathing patterns varied for individual singers performing different tasks, at different pitches, or in different registers. There is no information on whether breathing patterns were related to larynx height or whether there were differences in the accuracy of intonation between supported and unsupported voice. Griffin et al. (1995) did find that rib cage activity was greater than abdominal activity during the singing tasks in supported voice. Given the isolated nature of the tasks, however, it is difficult to draw any conclusions in relation to patterns of respiration and breath management; that would require the study of respiratory strategies used in connected song, both within whole phrases making different musical demands and between phrases.

The Griffin et al. (1995) study reported the majority of participants as referring only to breath management when describing production of the supported singing voice, while the experimental findings indicated that changes in laryngeal and glottal configuration, such as lowering the larynx and closing the glottis more tightly, played an important role in voice support. The study does, however, mention that six of the eight participants also included descriptions of inhalation (details are not given); three participants also referred specifically to posture and laryngeal or vocal tract involvement. Common pedagogical directions associated with inhalation, such as "breathing the start of the yawn," involve laryngeal and vocal tract adjustments, as do matters of posture. The fact that the majority of singers referred to these considerations and the fact that they were able to produce at will differences in voice quality between supported and unsupported voice, suggest that they were aware of factors other than respiration, even though they may have been unable to articulate this knowledge.

Another question raised by the Griffin et al. (1995) study, which needs extended investigation, is the differences between male and female voices, both in terms of anatomical and physiological characteristics and management strategies. The study found significant differences in many variables for gender, or pitch, or both. One finding was that subglottal pressure was higher in supported singing than unsupported singing for all voices except female low pitch. Because it is likely that the female low pitch (presumably sung in "chest register") had some overlap with the male high pitch (sung in "head register"), it would be interesting to know how this finding relates to register rather than to fundamental frequency in isolation. A marked difference was found between the amplitudes of the singer's formant in the supported and unsupported male voice. (The singer's formant is defined and discussed in Chapter 5.) It is not clear how this relates to the finding that men used more "compression of the larynx" and lowered the larynx more markedly than women, nor is it clear what this term means. If men used a lowered larynx high in their range, how did this affect laryngeal and respiratory strategies used to achieve the pitch and how did this compare with those adopted by women singing higher and with a higher larynx? Singing low in their range, did the women adopt similar strategies to those of the men singing high in their range?

Because of its importance in singing, subglottal pressure has been the focus of much research in recent years. Subglottal pressure may affect both loudness and pitch. In order to control intonation, particularly in loud singing, a singer needs fine control of subglottal pressure (Leanderson & Sundberg, 1988) because an increase in subglottal pressure may also, as a secondary effect, raise pitch (Sundberg, 1987). Many musical demands made of singers (for example, *messa di voce*, staccato, coordinated onset of phonation, leaps, and coloratura) require synchronized control between breathing muscles and pitch muscles (Astraquillo, Blatt, Happel, & Martinez, 1976; Proctor, 1980; Miller, 1986; Leanderson & Sundberg, 1988; Titze, 1992, 1996; Sundberg, 1993; Cleveland, 1994). Control of these coordinations is therefore of basic importance in singing, and understanding the factors involved and their interrelation is important for voice teachers.

Subglottal pressure depends on a complex system of passive recoil forces and active muscular forces. The demands on muscular forces to supply the required air pressure for phonation change continuously during singing as the music makes varying demands and as the recoil forces change with the lung volume. If the pressure generated by the recoil forces is too high for the intended phonation, then the inspiratory muscles must be contracted to reduce the pressure. The need for this activity then gradually decreases as the lung volume decreases until a lung volume is reached at which the passive recoil forces generate no pressure. Beyond this point, the muscles of exhalation must take over more and more to compensate for the increasing passive recoil force caused by the continuous compression of the rib cage (Leanderson & Sundberg, 1988).

A study by Leanderson, Sundberg, and von Euler (1987b) concluded that abdominal musculature contributes to the fast and dynamic control of subglottal pressure that is required for voice production. They reported this finding as being in contrast to the finding of Watson and Hixon (1985) (see earlier discussion) that the role of the abdominal muscles was "mainly one of posturing the chest wall," while "pressurization of the pulmonary system for singing, by contrast, appears to be the major role of the rib cage" (p. 119).

In a 1989 report, Watson, Hoit, Lansing, and Hixon described abdominal muscle activity during singing. They used electromyography at upper lateral, lower lateral, and midline sites of the abdomen to measure muscle activity during singing by four classical singers (bass, baritone, and bass-baritone). Muscle activity was found to be regional: The lateral region of the abdomen was highly active, whereas the middle region was not. Differential activation of the upper and lower portions of the lateral abdomen was also found, with the most common pattern showing greater activation of the lower portion than of the upper portion. Brief decrements in lateral abdominal activity often occurred in association with the onset of the inspiratory side of the breathing cycle. However, the investigators interpreted these findings on abdominal muscle activity as evidence that the abdominal muscles play an important role in the posturing of the chest wall for singing. The investigators were in turn critical of the fact that the Leanderson et al. (1987a) study used only single-site recordings.

Regardless of the conflicting interpretations the researchers put on the findings of these studies, from a practitioner point of view it seems that there is at least agreement that the abdominal muscles are important in controlling subglottal pressure. Because these studies used only male singers, the question arises whether the same breath management strategies apply to female singers.

The 1985 Watson and Hixon study used six male participants. In 1990, Watson, Hixon, Stathopoulos, and Sullivan did a similar study using four female participants. That investigation found no difference in kind between the kinematic behavior of the respiratory apparatus during the performance of these trained female classical singers and the comparable group of male classical singers studied earlier. This suggests that the same approach to respiratory training is appropriate for both male and female singers.

While both loudness and pitch are dependent on subglottal pressure, these factors are also influenced by airflow: Similar loudness can be achieved from a sound with reduced subglottal pressure and increased airflow, or from a sound with increased subglottal pressure and decreased airflow (Leanderson & Sundberg, 1988). As Cleveland put it, "The tradeoff between airflow and subglottal pressure is one directly related to the adductory force of the vocal folds" (1992, p. 26). He observed that trained classical singers seem to derive a louder sound with less subglottal pressure than untrained singers, which suggests that trained singers sing with less adductory force in the vocal folds than untrained singers. Efficiency of airflow in relation to vocal fold adduction results in flow phonation, rather than the breathy voice resulting from excessive airflow or the pressed voice resulting from insufficient airflow (Sundberg, 1987; Titze, 1994).

## Breath Management and Laryngeal Control

While it is sometimes useful to examine the component parts of the vocal mechanism (i.e., breath management, phonation, and resonance), I have already emphasized that for teachers of singing, whole-body use is of paramount importance. Issues of breath management are fundamental because of their influence on the whole of the vocal instrument. Some scientific studies involving respiration and other aspects of voice have been discussed above. In addition, three studies examining the influence of lung volume on laryngeal control are now considered.

A 1998 study of *messa di voce* is of immediate interest because it studied the physiological and acoustic characteristics of a vocal figure that many teachers prescribe as an exercise. The reason *messa di voce* is prescribed as an exercise is that it is quite common in vocal literature, and for a singer to execute it competently throughout the range requires practiced coordination. The gradual transition from pianissimo to fortissimo and back is a challenge to the singer's ability to change volume while keeping constant pitch, vowel, and timbre. Ideally, the crescendo and diminuendo halves of the figure are symmetrical. Titze et al. (1998) investigated whether the singers in their study were able to achieve this, and if there was an asymmetry in intensity, whether it could be attributed to a nonuniform depletion of lung volume. They also looked at whether there were problems at register transitions.

The participants were three male and three female singers covering a wide age range (25 to 61 years) and with varying performing experience (graduate student to ex-Metropolitan Opera soloist). The experimenters employed a method followed in earlier experiments, collecting data from a combination of transducers and electroglottograph. Each participant produced 27 tokens of the *messa di voce* over a range of about 1.5 octaves, each targeted to last 10 seconds— 5 seconds for the crescendo and 5 seconds for the diminuendo.

Rib cage displacement generally mirrored the lung volume rather closely, with abdomen displacement more variable. Sound pressure level was typically asymmetrical, with a delayed rise followed by an accelerated fall. Since the lung volume changes were generally quite linear throughout the exercise, this could not be attributed to a nonuniform expulsion of air. Variations in lung pressure and flow were seen in conjunction with variations in abdomen and rib cage displacement, suggesting that some differences in respiratory strategy seem to carry over to phonatory control. The participants displayed great variability in approach to "support," and there is no indication of which approach might be the most efficient in relation to phonatory control. While difficulties were identified in performing the exercise at higher pitches and (for the amateur tenor) at the register transition, stability of pitch, vowel, and timbre were not considered. Further studies are needed to shed more light on the complex coordinations required to execute a *messa di voce*.

In 1998, Iwarsson and collaborators published two studies. One (Iwarsson, Thomasson, & Sundberg, 1988) examined the effects of lung volume on the glottal voice source and the other (Iwarsson & Sundberg, 1998) the effects of lung volume on vertical larynx position during phonation. The study on glottal voice source followed up previous research that had raised the possibility that a variation in lung volume induces a variation of an abductive force component in the glottis. Because decreased abduction results in lower vocal fold vibration amplitude and longer closed phase, and hence a smaller amplitude of the airflow pulses through the glottis, it is obviously relevant to singing. Twenty-four untrained participants—14 men and 10 women—phonated at different pitches and degrees of vocal loudness at different lung volumes. Mean subglottal pressure was measured, and voice source characteristics were analyzed by inverse filtering. The investigation demonstrated that lung volume affects phonation: With decreasing lung volume, the closed quotient increased, while subglottal pressure, peak-to-peak flow amplitude, and glottal leakage tended to decrease. Based on these findings, the authors suggest that hyperfunctional voices might profit from phonation at high lung volumes, while for hypofunctional voices it may not be helpful to initiate phonation after a deep inhalation.

The study on vertical larynx position used a multichannel electroglottograph to measure larynx position in 29 healthy, vocally untrained participants—16 men and 13 women—who phonated at different lung volumes, pitches, and degrees of vocal loudness. High lung volume was found to be clearly associated with a lower larynx position, presumably one reason trained classical singers typically initiate phrases at high lung volumes.

## Application to Pedagogy

The physiology of respiration is complex, and the many interrelated aspects of breath management in singing are still being investigated. It seems that optimal breath management strategies may vary from singer to singer, depending on body type, and may also vary from one musical task to another.

Studies have highlighted the discrepancy between what singers believe they do to manage respiration and what they actually do. Watson and Hixon found that their highly trained and successful participants had "misconceptions ... concerning physical principles, some involving cause and effect, associated with respiratory physiology and mechanics" and "with regard to the function of the respiratory apparatus as a system" (1985, p. 119). They advocated

> additional emphasis in educating singers with regard to the workings of the respiratory apparatus and how such workings translate into performance. It seems reasonable to suppose that singers who have accurate conceptualizations about respiratory function would be in a better position to influence their performance product and use the respiratory apparatus more efficiently in performance. (p. 120)

Practitioners do not always agree. For example, Carroll and Sataloff (1991) maintained that the movement of the muscles of the lower abdomen, the upper abdomen and lower thorax, and the back that are involved in support should be inward and slightly upward, but "if teachers advise a student to bring abdominal muscles in and up, the student will also raise his or her shoulder, chest, and neck muscles" (p. 385). They suggested that the advice to support "down and out" is a matter of teaching imagery used to counter these unwanted muscular tensions (p. 386). Doscher (1994) was wary of using the term "support" at all, pointing out that the term suggests an inadvisable rigidity. She mentioned teachers successfully using "such imagery as feeling a cushion of air around the waist (patently physically impossible), of feeling the buoyancy of treading water, or of balancing lightly on a trampoline" (p. 24). Titze took a similar view in discussing approaches to teaching the coordinations that produce the appropriate airflow. He suggested using

> images that contain an ample number of the right physiological buzz-words. ... Thus, we could cushion the air with tone [sic], breathe the sound, connect the tone with the breath, or make the sound more or less airy, hooty, and fluty. The point is, we somehow want to make a connection between the laryngeal, pharyngeal, or oral sensations of airflow and the auditory perception of the sound produced. (Titze, 1994, p. 77)

In an issue of the *Journal of Voice* devoted to respiration and singing, R. C. White articulated two major responsibilities of singing teachers:

> The first is to achieve a thorough understanding of the physiological-mechanical processes through which the singing voice is produced. ... The second responsibility for teachers of singing is to formulate concepts based upon their understanding of the physiological-mechanical process and present them to students in terms *they* can understand and apply toward the development of a singing technique. (1988, p. 26)

Both White (1988) and Emmons (1988) asserted that in the studio most teachers use imagery to convey voice science understandings to students. Emmons argued that

> every teacher of singing accepts the fact that the possession of anatomically accurate information does not guarantee an effective *use* of air for singing. Frequently, a working concept (even an anatomically faulty one) is more useful (p. 30)

So may the teacher be led to look about for a way to control the thoracic and abdominal muscle groups *indirectly*, a way that would allow *them* to respond to the *task*, rather than to the specific controls of the singer. (p. 32)

An indirect approach to control is endorsed by the findings of Swank's 1984 investigation of verbal directives on support used by singing teachers and choral directors. Swank assumed that supported (i.e., well-sustained) tone would enable consistent tone quality from beginning to end, ability to sustain the integrity of the vowel over an extended period, and ability to maintain or increase the level of intensity over a period of time. She found that some directives had superior results at given pitches, while others showed superiority in solving another problem area of voice production. The most generally effective verbal directive was:

Following inhalation, press against the sternum with 2 fingers at the xiphoid process (lowest part of the sternum) and keep the *rib cage responding* to the *pressure* there throughout the sustained tone. Be conscious of the *expansion of the ribs at the sides* as you press with your fingers. (p. 14 )

This directive was based upon developing student awareness of raised rib cage, high sternum, and lateral expansion of ribs during the entire line of sustained sound, suggesting Titze's (1994) "pear-shape-up" posture. It was a directive based on physical awareness and was most effective at higher pitches. The next most effective directive was to "Sing *through* the *line* to end of the count, just as you would sing through the phrase of a song" (Swank, 1984, p. 13). This directive was most often issued with the intent of lessening tensions in singers and developing the concept of "flow" and "direction," while allowing the student to concentrate on the "end of the count." It was a directive based on mental control and was effective at lower pitches.

Swank concluded that "those directives which were most effective in this study encouraged postural aspects necessary to free and balanced respiratory technique for singing . . . and developed the concept of 'line' and breath as the carrier of tone" (1984, p. 17). This is an important point often neglected in scientific studies: From the pedagogical point of view, the correlation between body posture and breath management strategies is of primary importance.

While the studies by Watson and Hixon (1985) and Leanderson et al. (1987a) produced conflicting conclusions about the role of the diaphragm in controlled expiration in singing, both these studies demonstrated that singers were able to quickly learn new breath management strategies in response to visual feedback. In the Watson and Hixon study, one participant was able to train himself in the course of the experiment using observation of an oscilloscope. The researchers suggested that this may be a more efficient means of training respiratory behavior:

> Perhaps the use of only verbal instruction, visual example, and imagery in training singers should be discontinued. That is, it may be that in the case of respiratory function, at least, there is a useful role to be played by instrumentation of the type used in this investigation. (p. 120)

Leanderson et al. (1987a) reported that untrained participants were able to develop voluntary control of diaphragmatic activation in response to visual feedback, but pointed out that the trained participants had, without visual feedback, already developed such voluntary control during the course of their training. Visual feedback may be effective in speeding respiratory training.

The discussion above makes clear that breath management strategies influence phonation; issues of phonation are examined in greater detail in the following chapter.

## References

Allen, E., & Wilder, C. (1977). Respiratory patterns in singers: a proposed research design. In V. L. Lawrence (Ed.), *Transcripts of the sixth symposium on care of the professional voice* (pp. 18–20). New York: The Voice Foundation.

Astraquillo, C. J., Blatt, I. M., Happel, L., & Martinez, R. (1976). Investigation of the relationship between abdominal muscular discipline and the act of singing: an electromyographic study. *Annals of Otology, Rhinology and Laryngology, 84,* 498–519.

Brown, W. S., Hunt, E., & Williams, W. N. (1988). Physiological differences between the trained and untrained speaking and singing voice. *Journal of Voice, 2*(2), 102–110.

Brown, W. S., Rothman, H., & Williams, W. (1978). Physiological differentiation between singers and non-singers. In V. L. Lawrence (Ed.), *Transcripts of the seventh symposium on care of the professional voice, Pt I* (pp. 45–47). New York: The Voice Foundation.

Carroll, L. M., & Sataloff, R. T. (1991). The singing voice. In R. T. Sataloff (Ed.), *Professional voice. The science and art of clinical care* (pp. 381–401). New York: Raven Press.

Cleveland, T. F. (1992). Voice pedagogy for the twenty-first century: Physiological and acoustical basis for vocalises relating to subglottal pressure. *The NATS Journal, 49*(2), 25–26.

Cleveland, T. F. (1994). A clearer view of singing voice production: 25 years of progress. *Journal of Voice, 8*(1), 18–23.

Cleveland, T. F. (1998). A comparison of breath management strategies in classical and nonclassical singers. *Journal of Singing*, Part 1, *54*(5), 47–49; Part 2, *55*(1), 45–46; Part 3, *55*(2), 53–55.

Doscher, B. (1994). *The functional unity of the singing voice* (2nd ed.). Metuchen, NJ: Scarecrow Press.

Emmons, S. (1988). Breathing for singing. *Journal of Voice, 2*(1), 30–35.

Griffin, B., Woo, P., Colton, R., Casper, J., & Brewer, D. (1995). Physiological characteristics of the supported singing voice. A preliminary study. *Journal of Voice, 9*(1), 45–56.

Hixon, T., & Hoffman, C. (1979). Chest wall shape in singing. In V. L. Lawrence (Ed.), *Transcripts of the seventh symposium on care of the professional voice, Pt I* (pp. 9–10). New York: The Voice Foundation.

Hoit, J. D., Christie, L. J., Watson, P. J., & Cleveland, T. F. (1996). Respiratory function during speaking and singing in professional country singers. *Journal of Voice, 10*(1), 39–49.

Hoit, J. D., & Hixon, T. J. (1986). Body type and speech breathing. *Journal of Speech and Hearing Research, 29*, 313–324.

Iwarsson, J., & Sundberg, J. (1998). Effects of lung volume on vertical larynx position during phonation. *Journal of Voice, 12*(2), 159–165.

Iwarsson, J., Thomasson, M., & Sundberg, J. (1998). Effects of lung volume on the glottal voice source. *Journal of Voice, 12*(4), 424–433.

Leanderson, R., & Sundberg, J. (1988). Breathing for singing. *Journal of Voice, 2*(1), 2–12.

Leanderson, R., Sundberg, J., & von Euler, C. (1987a). Role of diaphragmatic activity during singing: a study of transdiaphragmatic pressures. *Journal of Applied Physiology, 62*, 259–270.

Leanderson, R., Sundberg, J., & von Euler, C. (1987b). Breathing muscle activity and subglottal pressure dynamics in singing and speech. *Journal of Voice, 1*(3), 258–261.

Leanderson, R., Sundberg, J., von Euler, C., & Lagercrantz, H. (1984). Diaphragmatic control of the subglottic pressure during singing. In V. L. Lawrence (Ed.), *Transcripts of the twelfth symposium, Care of the professional voice, 1983, Part II* (pp. 216–220). New York: The Voice Foundation.

McGlone, R. (1977). Supraglottal air pressure variation from trained singers while speaking and singing. In V. L. Lawrence (Ed.), *Transcripts of the sixth symposium on care of the professional voice* (pp. 48–49). New York: The Voice Foundation.

McKinney, J. C. (1982). *The diagnosis & correction of vocal faults.* Nashville, TN: Broadman Press.

Miller, R. (1977). *English, French, German and Italian techniques of singing: A study in national tonal preferences and how they relate to functional efficiency.* Metuchen, NJ: Scarecrow Press.

Miller, R. (1986). *The structure of singing. System and art in vocal technique.* New York: Schirmer Books.

Miller, R. (1999). The "sway-back" singer. Sotto voce. *Journal of Singing, 55*(3), 45–46.

Proctor, D. F. (1980). *Breathing, speech, and song.* Wien: Springer-Verlag.

Sataloff, R. T. (1992). The human voice. *Scientific American 267*(6), 108–115.

Sundberg, J. (1987). *The science of singing.* Dekalb, IL: Northern Illinois University Press.

Sundberg, J. (1993). Breathing behavior during singing. *The NATS Journal, 49*(3), 4–51.

Sundberg, J., Iwarsson, J., & Billström, A.-M. (1995). Significance of mechanoreceptors in the subglottal mucosa for subglottal pressure control in singers. *Journal of Voice, 9*(1), 20–26.

Sundberg, J., Leanderson, R., & von Euler, C. (1989). Activity relationship between diaphragm and cricothyroid muscles. *Journal of Voice, 3*(3), 225–232.

Swank, H. (1984). Some verbal directives regarding support concepts and their effects upon resultant sung tone. *The NATS Journal, 40*(3), 12–18.

Titze, I. R. (1992). Voice research: *Messa di voce. The NATS Journal, 48*(3), 24.

Titze, I. R. (1994). *Principles of voice production.* Englewood Cliffs, NJ: Prentice Hall.

Titze, I. R. (1996). Voice research: More on *messa di voce. Journal of Singing, 52*(4), 31–32.

Titze, I., Shirley, G., Long, R., Stathopoulos, E., Ramig, L., Carroll, L., & Riley, W. (1998). Messa di voce: An investigation of the symmetry of crescendo and decrescendo in a singing exercise, *NCVS Status and Progress Report* (KTH, Stockholm), *12*, 145–152.

Watson, P. J., & Hixon, T. J. (1985). Respiratory kinematics in classical (opera) singers. *Journal of Speech and Hearing Research, 28*, 104–122.

Watson, P. J., Hixon, T. J., Stathopoulos, E. T., & Sullivan, D. R.(1990). Respiratory kinematics in female classical singers. *Journal of Voice, 4*(2), 120–128.

Watson, P. J., Hoit, J. D., Lansing, R. W., & Hixon, T. J. (1989). Abdominal muscle activity during classical singing. *Journal of Voice, 3*(1), 24–31.

White, R.C. (1988). On the teaching of breathing for the singing voice. *Journal of Voice, 2*(1), 26–29.

# CHAPTER

# 4

# *Phonation*

The quality of the singing voice can only be as good as the voice source, the complex sound produced by the larynx. The operation of the larynx is affected by air pressure in the tube below (the trachea), the air column in the tube above (the vocal tract), the actions of the intrinsic muscles, the support provided by the extrinsic muscles, and the alignment of head and spine. The multilayered structure of the vocal folds is peculiarly suited to the delicate demands of phonation, with the cover and body acting as a double-structured vibrator. These small folds are, however, susceptible to strain through overuse, or through poor use due to inefficiencies in the larger system, respiratory infection, or dehydration. These factors, and possibly on-going repair of vocal fold tissue, account for the variability of ease of voice onset experienced by singers (Titze, 1998).

Over the last 25 years, technological developments have stimulated research into phonation. Nevertheless, it is still the case that theories about human laryngeal function are often of necessity extrapolated from research carried out on excised canine and feline larynges or inferred from mathematical models. As the least accessible part of the human vocal mechanism, the larynx still presents many puzzles. In 1988, Hirano admitted that

> the science is far behind the art. In spite of many investigations conducted by many researchers throughout the world, our knowledge of the vocal mechanism in singing is quite limited. There are two major bottlenecks: limitation in subjects and limitation in techniques. (Hirano, 1988, p. 69)

There has been some change since then: Researchers have developed more precise instrumentation and less invasive techniques, and therefore more singers are now willing to act as research subjects.

## Effect of Factors External to the Larynx

It is apparent that body alignment affects all aspects of singing. This is very clear in relation to laryngeal function. Given that the larynx, the hyoid bone, and the base of the tongue work as a physiological entity, anything that alters their relationship to each other and to the sternum, spinal column and skull affects phonation (Vilkman, Sonninen, Hurme, & Körkkö, 1996). The head needs to be positioned so that the sternocleidomastoid and scalene muscles can do their job of stabilizing the neck and thorax, and the external muscles contributing to voice production (the strap muscles, the cricopharyngeal, and thyropharyngeal) can work efficiently. With the exception of the cricopharyngeal muscle, the forces produced by the extrinsic laryngeal muscles act directly on the thyroid cartilage (Vilkman et al., 1996).

In Chapter 3, I mentioned that the posturing of the rib cage in relation to the abdomen adopted in different breath management strategies affects vocal control, partly through tracheal pull. Tracheal pull may increase the need for cricothyroid contraction and also reduce glottal adduction.

Then there is the unruly tongue. Because the tongue is attached to the hyoid bone, from which the larynx is suspended, the position of the tongue affects the larynx: Extending the tongue raises the larynx, and depressing the tongue lowers the larynx. Tension in the jaw also needs to be avoided, as it also affects the larynx through the muscles connected to the hyoid bone (the digastric, stylohyoid, mylohyoid, and geniohyoid).

## Onset

As a physical skill closely related to the musical aesthetics of singing, the onset of phonation is an aspect of vocal control which receives attention in most books on singing addressed to teachers and performers (see, for example, Vennard, 1967; Husler & Rodd-Marling, 1976; Miller, 1977, 1986; McKinney, 1982; Salaman, 1989; Bunch, 1995; Estill, 1996). Estill's model of voice training (1995, 1996) differs from many in addressing laryngeal skills in a quite mechanical way, through what she termed "compulsory figures" to achieve different modes of onset, retraction of the false vocal folds, vocal fold plane and mass, and laryngeal tilt.

Despite the practitioner's concern with onset, little experimental research has been centered on this aspect of the singing voice. Following Vennard's (1967) advocacy of the imaginary-aspirate onset as a technique to achieve balance between airflow and vocal fold adduction, Hirano (1971) investigated the muscular activity of three singers producing the "imaginary H" onset and three other types of onset: soft, hard, and breathy. For the "imaginary H" onset, in the leadup to phonation, gradually increasing activity was observed in cricothyroid, lateral cricoarytenoid, and vocalis muscles, with that activity reaching its maximum level around the vocal onset. The vocal initiation was not as slow as in the soft onset and not as abrupt as in the hard onset. There was no audible aspiration before onset. This mode of onset has been described by many practitioners as "simultaneous onset" (Doscher, 1994; Estill, 1996) or "balanced onset" (Miller, 1986); for classical styles, it is often advocated as being aesthetically pleasing and functionally more efficient than the extremes of breathy onset or glottal (hard) onset. It seems that it is favorable to establishing flow phonation.

As mentioned in the previous chapter, airflow at the glottis is determined by the interrelation of subglottic pressure and vocal fold resistance. Efficient coordination of these aspects of phonation produces maximum aerodynamic-to-acoustic energy conversion and minimum disturbance of the natural vibratory patterns of the vocal folds (flow phonation) (Titze, 1994). Flow phonation lessens mechanical stress on the laryngeal tissues and enables the production of vocal intensity with economical breath use (Gauffin & Sundberg, 1980; Sundberg, 1991).

The rate at which the airflow across the glottis decreases from maximum to minimum sets the overtone content of the voice source spectrum and also affects the overall amplitude of the sound (Sundberg, 1981; Sundberg, Titze, & Scherer, 1993). (The influence of laryngeal position on resonance factors is discussed further in Chapter 5.) When increased loudness, brightness, or excitement is called for, many singers tend toward pressed phonation. In this mode of phonation, the vocal processes are pressed together, reducing the average glottal aperture. The amplitude of vibration is relatively small and airflow is interrupted suddenly upon vocal fold collision and may produce irregularity in vocal fold vibration (Titze, 1992). A slightly spread posture of the vocal folds actually produces more power (Titze, 1994), with a convergent or near rectangular glottal configuration reducing the phonation threshold pressure to a minimum (Lucero, 1998). It is not intuitively obvious that this posture is advantageous; it is a learned skill (Titze, 1994).

While pressed phonation is not vocally efficient, neither is breathy phonation. The degree of acoustic interaction between the glottal source and the vocal tract is reduced when there is not a fairly complete glottal closure following the glottal flow pulse. Therefore, a voice that is breathy (in the sense that complete glottal closure is not attained during voicing) cannot develop the added carrying power that "inertive vocal tract loading" brings (Rothenberg, 1981). A longer closed phase means less acoustic energy is lost to the listener due to the coupling in of the subglottal cavities; less stored lung air is vented in each cycle, improving the efficiency of energy usage and enabling notes to be held for a longer time; and less breathiness of the voice quality (Howard, Lindsey, & Allen, 1990). Research by Howard, et al. and Howard (1995) found a positive correlation between the number of years of singing training and experience and the closed quotient. In men, closed quotient remained essentially constant with fundamental frequency, whereas in women closed quotient was reduced for pitches below $D_4$ and increased, with training, for pitches higher than $B_4$.

Research is beginning to explain the interactions between the form of the glottal flow pulses and the shape of the vocal tract (Ananthapadmanabha & Fant, 1982). Rothenberg (1981, 1983, 1984, 1987) suggested that the acoustic interaction between the glottal source and the vocal tract depends on an inertive force actualised by a momentary, inertia-induced increase in pressure in the trachea and a decrease in pressure in the pharynx caused by the inertia of the supraglottal air pulling it away from the closing glottis.

## Vibrato

It was previously thought that vocal vibrato was a phenomenon of the respiratory mechanism; recent studies have clarified that it is largely a phenomenon of the phonatory mechanism. Vibrato is, however, associated with movements of the articulatory apparatus and is perceived as an aspect of timbre. I have therefore chosen to discuss it in the following chapter, which deals with resonance.

## Control of Pitch

Pitch control rarely receives specific attention in texts on singing technique (Proctor, 1980 and Bunch, 1995 are exceptions). The implicit assumption is that if posture, audiation, breath management, onset,

and registration factors are under control, then the intended pitch will be produced.

There are three primary ways of regulating fundamental frequency: by contracting the cricothyroid muscles; by contracting the thyroarytenoid muscles; or by changing lung pressure to change the length, stiffness, and mass of the vocal folds (Titze, 1991). These mechanisms may, however, be interdependent. Frequency control may also involve vertical larynx position and larynx tilt, achieved by extrinsic laryngeal muscular activity.

Controlling either pitch or volume by lung pressure alone is inefficient, because these factors are interdependent. Fant (1985) maintained that the relative role of lung pressure as a determinant of voice output intensity has been overestimated and that "the abduction-adduction and other vocal cord activities carry the major part of the source dynamics, whilst lung pressure variations are slower and carry less information" (pp. 24–25). Hirano (1988) pointed out that the mechanism of intensity control is somewhat different in different registers and is also affected by fundamental frequency. These factors are further discussed in Chapter 6 in relation to registration.

Hirano's experiments have demonstrated that the activity of the cricothyroid, lateral cricoarytenoid, and vocalis muscles is positively related to fundamental frequency. The cricothyroid stretches and tenses the vocal fold, increasing fundamental frequency directly. The lateral cricoarytenoid stretches and tenses the vocal fold. The vocalis shortens the vocal fold and loosens the mucosa, which could be expected to decrease fundamental frequency, but when the vocalis contracts simultaneously with the cricothyroid, it may contribute to an increase in fundamental frequency (Hirano, 1988).

Further investigations into the regulation of fundamental frequency suggest that both positive and negative changes in fundamental frequency can occur with increased thyroarytenoid activity. At lower fundamental frequencies and lower vocal intensities, fundamental frequency correlates positively with thyroarytenoid activity, but at higher fundamental frequencies and low intensity (especially in falsetto voice), an increase in thyroarytenoid activity tends to lower fundamental frequency (Titze, Luschei, & Hirano, 1989).

Larynx height and tilt may also affect fundamental frequency control. The extrinsic laryngeal muscles are capable of changing the configuration of the structures important for fundamental frequency: the cricoid cartilage, the thyroid cartilage, and the hyoid bone (Erickson, Baer, & Harris, 1983). Investigations by Erickson et al. (1983) of the role of the strap muscles (extrinsic laryngeal muscles) in pitch lowering in speech found that a fall from high to low pitch was initiated by relaxation of the cricothyroid, with the strap muscles involved well after initiation of the frequency fall. A fall from mid to low pitch, however, was initiated by the strap muscles, with the cricothyroid playing a relatively small role.

In 1975, Shipp and Izdebski found that inexperienced singers used upward (from rest) larynx position for higher voice frequency, presumably to accomplish an increase in vocal fold stretching in a vertical plane to supplement the horizontal pulling forces provided by dorsocaudal tilting of the cricoid cartilage. Experienced singers, on the other hand, tended to maintain larynx position near or well below the physiological resting level as they raised frequency, presumably utilizing almost exclusively the horizontal pulling forces provided by cricothyroid muscle contraction. This latter strategy maintains supraglottal resonator configuration. A further investigation by Shipp (1977) concluded that while it may require less effort to produce high frequencies by elevating the larynx, voice quality suffers. Sundberg and Askenfelt's 1981 study supported this finding. They found larynx rise to be associated with an upward shift in the formant frequencies but, generally, also a decrease in the amplitude of the source spectrum fundamental and in the amplitude of the vibrato undulations. Thus, vertical laryngeal position affects both phonation and resonance.

## Pitch Matching

Experiments in vocal matching of pitch patterns (Leonard & Ringel, 1979; Leonard, Ringel, Horii, & Daniloff, 1988) have found a direct relationship between interval size and speed of matching. Leonard and collaborators (1979, 1988) also found pitch lowering to be faster than pitch raising, with singers faster and more accurate than non-singers. The participants in these experiments were all men with baritone or bass voices, singing in modal register. Sundberg's 1979 investigation of speed of pitch changes used equal numbers of male and female participants. His results confirmed the findings of Leonard and collaborators: Trained singers were able to change pitch faster than untrained subjects; the greater the pitch rise, the slower the response time; and pitch drops were performed faster than pitch elevations (at least by untrained subjects). He also found that women tended to perform pitch changes faster than men. Untrained subjects used larynx height to achieve pitch changes, whereas trained subjects maintained a relatively stable larynx position in order to maintain the singer's formant. (The influence of laryngeal position on resonance factors is discussed further in Chapter 5.) The results did not support the view that larynx height alterations increase the speed of pitch changes.

The usual assumption is that singers' superior pitch-matching ability is associated with superior auditory awareness. Sundberg (1979) proposed that it may also depend on the fact that singers have developed more precise cricothyroid muscle control and a "muscle memory" appropriate to the task. Among singers in this investigation, pitch changes of a given direction tended to be synchronized with the phase of the vibrato cycle that changed the frequency in the same direction, probably controlled at least in part by the auditory feedback system.

## Intrinsic Pitch of Vowels

Another issue involved in fundamental frequency is what has been called the intrinsic pitch of vowels. Sapir (1989) pointed out that high vowels such as /i/ and /u/ tend to be produced with higher fundamental frequency than low vowels such as /ɑ/, even in the same phonetic context and that this effect has been demonstrated in normal speech, in singing, and in the speech of deaf speakers. Knowledge of singing technique and articulatory and acoustic phonetics would lead to the assumption that such a phenomenon is related to tongue position. Sapir also reported several rival hypotheses, however, based on different types of coupling between the articulatory and the phonatory systems: acoustic coupling, mechanical coupling, and neural coupling. In his assessment of the then-available data, Sapir concluded that the evidence was insufficient to establish which mechanism or combination of mechanisms is responsible for the intrinsic pitch of vowels.

Vilkman, Sonninen, Hurme, and Körkkö (1996) suggested the longitudinal tension of the vocal folds is changed by the cricothyroid muscle as a reflex-like compensation to vertical articulatory movements such as tongue and palate heightening and lowering of the larynx.

For practitioners, the important consideration is how to compensate for the intrinsic pitch of vowels. Sapir (1989) postulated that singers may achieve better fundamental frequency control by adopting strategies that decouple the articulatory and phonatory systems. He suggested restricting vertical laryngeal movements for vowel production and assuming the oral postures least likely to affect laryngeal tension. Sapir's research, and that on pitch matching described above, supported the received wisdom of singing pedagogy that articulatory maneuvers should not be allowed to interfere with the phonatory mechanism.

Singers' superior control of fundamental frequency seems to result at least in part from training and experience (Murry, 1990), although it is not clear what innate abilities may be involved (Murry & Zwirner, 1991). No doubt training and experience contribute to singers' ability to achieve the balance between subglottal pressure and vocal fold stiffening involved in pitch and dynamic changes. Practitioners use the traditional *messa di voce* exercise (singing the same pitch, while the loudness is varied from soft to loud and then back to soft, with no change in timbre) to cultivate this coordination (Cleveland, 1992; Titze, 1996).

Music psychologists suggest that pitch-matching accuracy relates to the perceived musical relevance of the task and the quality of feedback available. As in other aspects of vocal development, real-time visual feedback has been shown to be effective in improving pitch matching (Welch, Howard, & Rush, 1989; Howard & Welch, 1993).

## References

Ananthapadmanabha, T. V., & Fant, G. (1982). Calculation of true glottal flow and its components. *Speech Communication, 1,* 167–184.

Bunch, M. (1995). *Dynamics of the singing voice* (3rd ed.). Wien: Springer-Verlag.

Cleveland, T. F. (1992). Voice pedagogy for the twenty-first century: Physiological and acoustical basis for vocalises relating to subglottal pressure. *The NATS Journal, 49*(2), 25–26.

Doscher, B. (1994). *The functional unity of the singing voice* (2nd ed.). Metuchen, NJ: Scarecrow Press.

Erickson, D., Baer, T., & Harris, K. S. (1983). The role of the strap muscles in pitch lowering. In D. M. Bless & J. H. Abbs (Eds.), *Vocal fold physiology: Contemporary research and clinical issues* (pp. 279–285). San Diego, CA: College-Hill Press.

Estill, J. (1995). *Voice craft. A user's guide to voice quality. Vol. 2: Some basic voice qualities.* Santa Rosa, CA: Estill Voice Training Systems.

Estill, J. (1996). *Voice craft. A user's guide to voice quality. Level One: Primer of compulsory figures.* Santa Rosa, CA: Estill Voice Training Systems.

Fant, G. (1985). Acoustic parameters of the voice source. In A. Askenfelt, S. Felicetti, E. Jansson, & J. Sundberg (Eds.), *Proceedings of the Stockholm Music Acoustics Conference, 1983, Vol. 1* (pp. 11–26). Sweden: Royal Swedish Academy of Music.

Gauffin, J., & Sundberg, J. (1980). Data on the glottal source behavior in vowel production. *Speech Transmission Laboratory Quarterly Progress Status Report* (KTH, Stockholm), 2–3, 61–70.

Hirano, M. (1971). Laryngeal adjustment for different vocal onset. *Journal of otolaryngology of Japan, 74,* 1572–1579.

Hirano, M. (1988). The G. Paul Moore Lecture. Vocal mechanisms in singing: Laryngological and phoniatric aspects. *Journal of Voice, 1*(1), 51–69.

Howard, D. M. (1995). Variation of electrolaryngographically derived closed quotient for trained and untrained adult female singers. *Journal of Voice, 9*(2), 163–172.

Howard, D. M., Lindsey, G. A., & Allen, B. (1990). Toward the quantification of vocal efficiency. *Journal of Voice, 4*(3), 205–212.

Howard, D. M., & Welch, G. F. (1993). Visual displays for assessment of vocal pitch matching development. *Applied Acoustics, 39,* 235–252.

Husler, F., & Rodd-Marling, Y. (1976). *Singing. The physical nature of the vocal organ.* London: Hutchinson.

Leonard, R. J., & Ringel, R. L. (1979). Vocal shadowing under conditions of normal and altered laryngeal sensation. *Journal of Speech and Hearing Research, 22*(4), 794–817.

Leonard, R. J., Ringel, R., Horii, Y., & Daniloff, R. (1988). Vocal shadowing in singers and nonsingers. *Journal of Speech and Hearing Research, 31,* 54–61.

Lucero, J. (1998). Optimal glottal configuration for ease of phonation. *Journal of Voice, 12*(2), 151–158.

McKinney, J. C. (1982). *The diagnosis & correction of vocal faults.* Nashville, TN: Broadman Press.

Miller, R. (1977). *English, French, German and Italian techniques of singing: A study in national tonal preferences and how they relate to functional efficiency.* Metuchen, NJ: Scarecrow Press.

Miller, R. (1986). *The structure of singing. System and art in vocal technique.* New York: Schirmer Books.

Murry, T. (1990). Pitch-matching accuracy in singers and nonsingers. *Journal of Voice, 4*(4), 317–321.

Murry, T., & Zwirner, P. (1991). Pitch matching ability of experienced and inexperienced singers. *Journal of Voice, 5*(3), 197–202.

Proctor, D. F. (1980). *Breathing, speech, and song.* Wien: Springer-Verlag.

Rothenberg, M. (1981). The voice source in singing. In J. Sundberg (Ed.), *Research aspects on singing* (pp. 15–28). Stockholm: The Royal Swedish Academy of Music.

Rothenberg, M. (1983). An interactive model for the voice source. In D. M. Bless, & J. H. Abbs (Eds.), *Vocal fold physiology: Contemporary research and clinical issues* (pp. 155–165). San Diego, CA: College-Hill Press.

Rothenberg, M. (1984). Source-tract acoustic interaction and voice quality. In V. L. Lawrence (Ed.), *Transcripts of the twelfth symposium, Care of the professional voice, 1983, Pt I* (pp. 25–31). New York: The Voice Foundation.

Rothenberg, M. (1987). Così fan tutte and what it means, or Nonlinear source-tract acoustic interaction in the soprano voice and some implications for the definition of vocal efficiency. In T. Baer, C. Sasaki, & K. S. Harris (Eds.), *Laryngeal function in phonation and respiration* (pp. 254–267). Boston: College-Hill Press.

Salaman, E. (1989). *Unlocking your voice. Freedom to sing.* London: Victor Gollancz.

Sapir, S. (1989). The intrinsic pitch of vowels: Theoretical, physiological, and clinical considerations. *Journal of Voice, 3*(1), 44–51.

Shipp, T. (1977). Vertical laryngeal position in singing. *Journal of Research in Singing, 1*(1), 16–24.

Shipp, T., & Izdebski, K. (1975). Vocal frequency and vertical larynx positioning by singers and nonsingers. *Journal of the Acoustical Society of America, 58*(5), 1104–1106.

Sundberg, J. (1979). Maximum speed of pitch changes in singers and untrained subjects. *Journal of Phonetics, 7,* 71–79.

Sundberg, J. (1981). The voice as a sound generator. In J. Sundberg (Ed.), *Research aspects on singing* (pp. 6–14). Stockholm: The Royal Swedish Academy of Music.

Sundberg, J. (1991). Comparisons of pharynx, source, formant and pressure characteristics in operatic and musical theatre singing. *Speech Transmission Laboratory Quarterly Progress Status Report* (KTH, Stockholm), 2–3, 51–62.

Sundberg, J., & Askenfelt, A. (1981). Larynx height and voice source. A relationship? *Speech Transmission Laboratory Quarterly Progress Status Report* (KTH, Stockholm), 2–3, 23–36.

Sundberg, J., Titze, I., & Scherer, R. (1993). Phonatory control in male singing: A study of the effects of subglottal pressure, fundamental frequency, and mode of phonation on the voice source. *Journal of Voice, 7*(1), 15–29.

Titze, I. R. (1991). Mechanisms underlying the control of fundamental frequency. In J. Gauffin & B. Hammarberg (Eds.), *Vocal fold physiology. Acoustic, perceptual, and physiological aspects of voice mechanisms* (pp. 129–138). San Diego, CA: Singular Publishing Group.

Titze, I. R. (1992). Voice research: Voice Quality: Part 1. *The NATS Journal, 48*(5), 21, 45.

Titze, I. R. (1994). *Principles of voice production.* Englewood Cliffs, NJ: Prentice Hall.

Titze, I. R. (1996). Voice research: More on *messa di voce. Journal of Singing, 52*(4), 31–32.

Titze, I. R. (1998). Voice research: On the springiness and stickiness of vocal fold tissues. *Journal of Singing, 54*(5), 35–36.

Titze, I. R., Luschei, E. S., & Hirano, M. (1989). Role of the thyroarytenoid muscle in regulation of fundamental frequency. *Journal of Voice, 3*(3), 213–224.

Vennard, W. (1967). *Singing—The mechanism and the technic* (rev. ed.). New York: Carl Fischer.

Vilkman, E., Sonninen, A., Hurme, P., & Körkkö. (1996). External laryngeal frame function in voice production revisited: A review. *Journal of Voice, 10*(1), 78–92.

Welch, G. F., Howard, D. M., & Rush, C. (1989). Real-time visual feedback in the development of vocal pitch accuracy in singing. *Psychology of Music, 17,* 146–157.

# CHAPTER 5

# *Resonance and Articulation*

**A**s I emphasized in Chapter 4, the quality of the voice depends essentially on the voice source. It also depends on how that spectrum of sound is filtered by the vocal tract. Even the level of the fundamental is dependent not only on the voice source, but also on the vocal tract filtering and the characteristics of the sound radiation from the lip opening (Gauffin & Sundberg, 1989). As discussed in the previous chapter, however, articulatory adjustments (for both timbre and word articulation) need to be achieved without compromising the voice source: Voice source and vocal tract filter are interdependent, just as subglottal pressure and laryngeal adjustment are interdependent.

Pedagogical concerns about resonance and articulation include production of the timbre appropriate to the musical context, vowel quality, vibrato, and articulation of text. Vocal resonance and word articulation are interdependent parameters reliant on the movements of the articulators. It is with respect to these interdependent parameters that an understanding of the relationship between physical maneuvers and acoustic results is vital for pedagogy.

The traditional identification of different vowels with particular emotions and vocal color (as discussed, for example, in Vennard, 1967 and Manén, 1987) is supported by acoustic findings. Each vowel sound corresponds to a characteristic pattern of articulator adjustment. Each articulation also corresponds to a combination of formant frequencies characteristic of that vowel. In teaching, the singer does much tuning of formant frequencies intuitively by attention to vowel quality and the emotional motivation of a text, with the teacher supplying the analytical ear able to identify articulatory problems causing acoustic distortion. The danger is that one fixed configuration of articulators may be seen as correct, militating against the subtle adjustments necessary to maintain acoustic balance while the relative dimensions of the vocal tract resonators change in response to phonetic articulation (Miller, 1986).

## Vowels and Resonance

Vowel production for speech involves the shape of the lips, the opening between the jaws, the position of the soft palate, and the shape of the tongue. Classification of vowels, however, has usually been done by reference only to the position of the main body of the tongue in the oral cavity: high-low and front-back (O'Connor, 1973; Denes & Pinson, 1993). In the traditional vowel triangle, /i/ is at the high front corner, /u/ at the high back corner, and /ɑ/ at the low back corner. Titze (1997) likened these vowels to primary colors, in that the articulatory space defined by these "corner vowels" defines that required for the vowels in many (if not all) languages. Other vowels, such as the neutral /ʌ/ and /ə/ vowels, are classified as central. Vowels may also be classified as "closed" (the tongue near the palate) or "open" (the tongue low, at the bottom of the mouth) (Denes & Pinson, 1993).

In moving from speaking to singing, vowels are modified to produce a wider dynamic range (both for artistry and to be heard), to maintain a balance in loudness across phonemes, and in order to produce particular vocal timbres (Titze, 1995). In this modification, many combinations of articulatory adjustment may be involved, allowing shifts in formant frequencies and subtle adjustments to timbre and vowel quality. Recent research has increased understanding of how articulatory adjustments are used in formant tracking and in production of the singer's formant.

## Control of Formant Frequencies

The first formant is particularly affected by the mandible, the second formant by the tongue shape, and the third formant by the position of the tip of the tongue or, when the tongue is retracted, to the size of the cavity between the lower incisors and the tongue (Sundberg, 1991a).

These principles have been elaborated by Pickett (1980) as rules for the modification of formant frequencies by specific articulatory maneuvers. Pickett's first rule is that all formant frequencies decrease uniformly as the length of the vocal tract increases. The second rule is that all formant frequencies decrease uniformly with lip rounding and increase with lip spreading. In combination with larynx height adjustments, lip rounding or spreading can be effective in darkening or brightening the vowels.

Pickett lays down two additional rules for when either the front half of the vocal tract (the mouth) or the back half (the pharynx) is narrowed in relation to the other half. His third rule is this: A front constriction (e.g., raising the tongue toward the roof of the mouth, as in the phoneme /i/) lowers the first formant and raises the second formant. This creates a more diffuse sound across the frequency spectrum. More acoustic energy is spread out over both low and high frequencies. The fourth rule states that a back constriction raises the first formant and lowers the second formant, making the overall sound more compact in the middle part of the frequency spectrum, as in the case of an /ɑ/ vowel. A constriction in the center of the vocal tract, as in /u/, does not affect the formant frequencies, but the large degree of lip rounding lowers both first and second formant for /u/.

Titze (1998) pointed out that widening the pharynx produces a darker, stronger sound quality. The first formant frequency is lowered, and the vocal tract emphasizes lower partials. For the vowel to be identified, however, the location and degree of constriction of the vocal tract characteristic of the vowel must remain relative to the mouth configuration. For example, for a vowel to be perceived as /ɑ/, the vocal tract must be more constricted in the pharynx than in the mouth.

Vocal intensity can be significantly increased by tuning formants of the vocal tract to harmonics of the source (Titze, 1991). A singer may use what Titze (1995) called the "megaphone effect" produced by lowering the jaw and moving the lips forward and inward at the corners of the lips. This maneuver both widens and lengthens the vocal tract, producing a louder sound.

Increasing acoustic output power with formant tuning is very sensitive to fundamental frequency (Titze, 1984). In a landmark investigation of the pitch-dependent changes in lip and jaw opening made in a professional soprano, Sundberg (1975) found that the formant frequencies were similar to those of normal speech only when the fundamental was lower in frequency than the first formant. When the fundamental rose to a higher value, dropping and retracting the jaw and spreading the lips shifted the frequency of the first formant upwards close to the fundamental. This maneuver achieves an amplification of the vocal source far more economically than would be possible using subglottal pressure. Using this strategy, however, causes the formant frequency differences between the vowels to gradually disappear as the fundamental frequency increases, resulting in the well-known phenomenon of words being difficult to distinguish when sung at high pitch in operatic style.

Subsequent studies (Bloothooft & Plomp, 1984, 1985; Scotto di Carlo & Rutherford, 1990; Gottfried & Chew, 1992; Johansson, Sundberg, & Wilbrand, 1992; Smith & Scott, 1992) confirmed the finding of decreasing intelligibility with rising pitch. Both Gottfried and Chew (1992) and Smith and Scott (1992) found that intelligibility was improved by the presence of consonantal transitions. Smith and Scott (1992) suggested that the generally accepted notion that vowel sounds are largely unintelligible on higher notes pertains only to a restricted manner of production (i.e., operatic voice quality). They found isolated vowels sung with raised larynx to be more intelligible than isolated vowels sung in operatic quality, and vowels sung with high larynx and consonantal transitions to be even more intelligible.

Lindestad and Södersten (1988) found that in singing at high pitch, their four countertenor subjects employed a different strategy from that reported for sopranos. Using countertenor voice, the subjects sang fundamental frequencies of 662, 524, and 494 Hz, all frequencies higher than the normal value of the first formant frequency in men. Rather than using jaw opening to raise the first formant, they achieved this effect by shortening the vocal tract by means of larynx raising and "lower pharynx" (presumably laryngopharynx) narrowing. The researchers noted a great deal more pharyngeal activity in connection with variations in pitch and intensity in the countertenor than in the baritone singing of the subjects, notably a clear change in the configuration of the laryngeal tube when changing from modal voice to countertenor phonation, with a widening at the level of the ventricular folds. This may have been because the countertenors were not as accomplished in the baritone range of the voice, or because they did not cultivate the singer's formant in the baritone range in order to achieve a better match in timbre with the countertenor sound.

In a more recent study, Sundberg and Skoog (1996) measured the jaw opening in 10 professional male and female singers of different voice types as they sang an ascending two-octave scale on different vowels after determining the normal first formant frequency at a relatively low pitch. Each of the singers (one bass, two baritones, two tenors, one mezzo soprano/alto, two mezzo sopranos, and one soprano) sang six vowels (/a/, /ɑ/, /o/, /u/, /i/, /e/) at 25 pitches.

They found that only for the vowels /a/ and /ɑ/ did the singers widen the jaw opening as the fundamental frequency approached that of the first formant. For the other vowels, the jaw was widened at higher pitches. In those vowels, the singer can increase the first formant by reducing tongue constriction.

Several researchers (e.g., Miller & Schutte, 1990; Carlsson & Sundberg, 1992) have noted Coffin's system of singing training based on tuning the vocal tract. Coffin's *Sounds of Singing* (1987) and *Overtones of Bel Canto* (1980), and the "Chromatic vowel chart for voice building and tone placing" in the later publication, were built on the premise that "while spoken vowel values vary according to languages and dialects, in singing they *cannot* depart from the coincidence of a vowel pitch and an harmonic of the sung pitch. This is an *absolute* of singing" (1987, p. 4). Coffin's system is essentially a documentation of traditional pedagogies (he quotes Lamperti, Mancini, Tosi, Garcia, Marchesi, Lilli Lehmann, and Nicolai Gedda's teacher, Paola Novikova) with the purpose of showing "how to bring the frequencies of the vocal cords and the vocal tract into concord on the various notes and vowels" (1987, p. 45). The vowel chart is a system of "vowel shading" (i.e., modification expressed in terms of color) "for louder resonance." It shows quite specific vowel modifications for specific pitches, related to vocal registration for a range of voice types and notes the general rule that "low notes should be brightened to accentuate the high harmonics so the voice can be heard. ... High notes should be rounded in all voices to place energy in the lower harmonics" (Coffin, 1987, Chromatic Vowel Chart). An essential aspect of the system is identification of *passaggi* for the different voice types and an interpretation of "high notes" and "low notes" in relation to these voice types.

Miller and Schutte (1990) examined the amplifying power of formant tuning employed by a baritone in the range of 230 to 380 Hz (roughly B-flat$_3$ to F$_4$), a range traversing the *primo passaggio*. The baritone used different strategies, depending on the musical context. In a rising arpeggio spanning the octave from B-flat$_3$, sung on /bi- bi- bi- bi-/, the singer produced notes of considerable intensity by tuning the formants to match one of the low harmonics. In singing a descending scale passage from F$_4$ to B-flat$_3$ on the vowel /i/ after a /b/ onset, there was little vowel modification and the first formant stayed close to the fundamental. Presumably the combination of rising pitch and plosives required increasing subglottal pressure for the rising arpeggio, causing formant tuning to be employed to maintain uniform intensity. This, as well as the fact that it traversed the *passaggio*, required vowel modification. In the descending scale passage, on the other hand, subglottal pressure was not an issue, and the closeness of the intervals with no intervening consonant would make vowel distortion obvious.

Carlsson and Sundberg (1992) had a similar finding in relation to synthesized "singing" of a descending chromatic scale. They found that an expert panel preferred constant formant frequencies to formant tuning, presumably because of the shifts in vowel quality between adjacent notes that formant tuning causes.

The relationship of formant tuning (vowel modification) to the singer's formant and to vocal registration is discussed below.

### The Singer's Formant

There has long been interest in what produces the exciting ringing quality of the professional singing voice, the quality that gives an arresting "edge" to the voice. This quality—the singer's formant—assists register blending and legato line and is essential for singers to be heard clearly over large orchestras, electronic instruments, or background noise. For these reasons, much of the literature on vocal technique in singing contains directions on how to achieve brilliance or "ring" (e.g., Vennard, 1967).

In his pioneering work in the 1960s, Vennard (1967, p. 166) stated that the singer's formant results when "the resonators are in tune with the vibrator," that is, when the resonators are shaped to reinforce vowel formants that are harmonics of the fundamental. The most common way of tuning formant frequencies is to adjust the vocal tract shape by moving the articulators. Constricting the vocal tract in the glottal region also leads to an increase of the formant frequencies. If the third, fourth, and fifth formats are close in frequency, thus forming a formant cluster, the singer's formant peak can be explained as an articulatory phenomenon that can be produced with a normal voice source. Clustering of formants can be attained if the pharynx is wide in comparison with the entrance to the larynx tube. This tube, immediately above the vocal folds, is about 2 cm long, with its anterior wall formed by the epiglottis and the posterior wall by the arytenoid cartilages (Sundberg, 1995).

Sundberg (1991a) has identified the singer's formant as an exceptionally high spectrum envelope peak appearing in the vicinity of 3 kHz in all vowel spectra. The acoustic effect may be reinforced by the fact that the frequencies in the 3 kHz range are those most easily perceived by the human ear. The center frequency of the singer's formant is around 2.2 kHz for basses, around 2.7 for baritones, around 2.8 for tenors, and around 3.2 for altos. Sundberg suggested that in sopranos, it is nothing but a perfectly normal third and fourth formant. Nevertheless, the perceptual effect of clear, ringing quality independent of vowel or pitch is certainly present in accomplished soprano singing.

Since the invention of instrumentation for objective voice analysis, voice science has been able to offer some explanations of the singer's formant. A series of investigations by Sundberg found that the singer's formant is resonated by a complex cavity produced by the expansion of the laryngeal ventricle, pyriform sinuses, and laryngopharyx. Sundberg found that this cavity requires a low larynx and a wide pharynx leading to a narrowed larynx tube, with the widened pharynx being six times the area of the opening to the larynx tube (Sundberg, 1974, 1977, 1981, 1983, 1987, 1991b, 1995).

Detweiler (1994) tested Sundberg's hypothesis on three classically trained professional male singers. The singers did produce the singer's formant, but without achieving the laryngopharyngeal/laryngeal outlet cross-sectional area ratio requisite to Sundberg's model. They also sang with varying laryngeal height. Detweiler pointed out that these data on larynx height are consistent with the data of Shipp and Izdebski (1975) (discussed in Chapter 4), Wang (1985), Sengupta (1990), and Dmitriev and Kiselev (1979). She maintained that the laryngeal system as modeled by Sundberg is not the resonance source of the singer's formant in these subjects and postulates that the singer's formant is an aggregate formant constituted by the combined resonances of two component formants. The position is similar to that taken by Simonson (1987), who investigated the acoustic effects on the singer's formant of tuning the first formant with the fundamental. He found effective increases in intensity of both the first formant and the singer's formant by placing the fundamental and the first formant in a harmonic relationship.

Responding to Detweiler's work, Sundberg (1995) measured the formant frequency changes due to a doubling of the cross-sectional area at each 0.5 cm interval along the vocal tract length axis, in order to test the assumption that the fourth formant is strongly dependent on the larynx tube. He found that the fourth and fifth formants were very sensitive to the details of the area function of the larynx tube. His results supported the assumption that the singer's formant is strongly, though not entirely, associated with the larynx tube. He made the point that more accurate assessment requires sweep frequency measurements of high fidelity, three-dimensional models of the vocal tract.

Sundberg's 1995 study also attempted to quantify how prominent the spectrum envelope peak at the level near 3 kHz needs to be to qualify as a singer's formant. The formant levels were mathematically predicted, and these predictions were compared with data collected from singers in an anechoic chamber. Four tenors and four baritones or basses, all professional opera singers, sang a vowel sequence with the consonant /v/ interspersed between the vowels. Three sopranos sang the solo part of Felix Mendelssohn's motet *Hear My Prayer*.

All male singers showed a clear singer's formant. For the sopranos, the result was varied. In some cases a given vowel showed a strong singer's formant, and in other cases the singer's formant was absent. The singer's formant is said to be a phenomenon of the operatic voice; Sundberg does not explain why singing tasks so different in kind were set for men and women, nor why the repertoire selected for the sopranos was from oratorio rather than opera and from a piece frequently performed by the boy treble voice. It is likely that such a choice would have affected the vocal quality employed by the subjects.

Most work on the singer's formant has assumed a "classical" Western timbre. Wang (1985), however, studied larynx position in 10 tenors singing in three different styles, Western operatic, Chinese, and that used for Western early music, all showing "bright timbre." He found the singer's formant in conjunction with low larynx in the Western operatic style and in conjunction with high larynx in Chinese and early music singers. While Wang's findings have been questioned (Sundberg, 1991a), it is still of interest that the voice qualities used in many different musics may contain the singer's formant as part of their acoustic profile. Sengupta's investigation of some acoustic features of North Indian classical singing identified the singer's formant in both male and female singers. He found that the center frequency of the singer's formant increased with rising pitch, as has been found in other vocal qualities (Sengupta, 1990).

Perceptually, the vocal quality of these styles has much in common with that loud, "twangy" sound usually labeled "belting" by Western practitioners. "Twang" is one aspect of a number of vocal qualities. Yanagisawa, Estill, Kmucha, and Leder (1989) attributed "twang" to constriction of the aryepiglottic sphincter. They found that when the aryepiglottic sphincter is constricted, it creates an extra resonator between the aryepiglottic rim and the vocal folds, raising the partials in the 3 kHz area of the spectrum. This resembles Sundberg's theory (1987, 1995) that a wide pharynx and narrowed larynx tube are prerequisites for production of the singer's formant.

For a voice to have a strong ringing quality, there must also be a stronger-than-average distribution of high frequency energy in the glottal airflow pulses entering the vocal tract from the glottis; this energy is generated by the acoustic interaction between the glottal source and the inertance present in the subglottal and supraglottal

airflow (Rothenberg, 1984). The sharp cutoff of airflow that is characteristic of the glottal wave is an important source of the high-frequency components of the glottal source spectrum. It is also possible to sharpen the cutoff by adjusting the mechanical properties of the vocal folds (Baken, 1991). The creation of the high-frequency components of the voice source is thus dependent on both trans-glottal flow and laryngeal adjustment.

Howard, Lindsey, and Allen (1990) found that if the closed phase of the vocal fold vibratory cycle is increased, due to the coupling in of the subglottal cavities, less acoustic energy is lost to the listener. By increasing the closed quotient, the professional singer increases overall system efficiency: An increase in output acoustic energy associated with a decrease in the expenditure of stored input energy is a natural acoustic consequence of adjusting how the folds vibrate. Titze (1986) pointed out that not only does a constriction above the vocal folds followed by an expansion in the pharynx resonate the partials around 3 kHz, but the constriction itself causes the larynx to produce more energy in the higher partials, producing a kind of feedback effect. It also achieves an acoustic decoupling of the vocal folds from the influence of changing vowels (Titze & Story, 1977).

Reid (1990) emphasized the interrelationship between "close cavity coupling," in which resonance at larynx level is reinforced by pharyngeal configuration, and the importance of the larynx as a regulator of the amplitude of sound waves introduced into the vocal tract. He identified narrowing of the ventricular folds as an essential element in creating a buildup of supraglottal pressure and regulating the amount of energy introduced into adjacent resonators.

In summary, current research indicates that production of the singer's formant is associated with a long closed phase in the vocal fold vibratory cycle, narrowing of the vocal tract immediately above the larynx, a wide pharynx, and adjustment of the articulators to maximize close cavity coupling. It may also involve aryepiglottic constriction and narrowing of the ventricular folds.

A study by Teie (1976) confirmed the assumption that for the majority of singers, the ability to produce the singer's formant is learned. He compared the characteristics of the singer's formant in the voice spectra of male and female singers at four levels: untrained singers, first year college voice students, fourth year college voice students, and mature singers (voice faculty). The only statistically significant differences in the intensity peaks of the singer's formant among groups were found between the untrained singers and the trained singers. No statistically significant differences were found among the trained singer groups.

Findings on the center frequency of the singer's formant in the different voice types suggest the possibility of classifying voices by objective formant analysis.

## Nasal Resonance Versus Brilliance

Many pedagogies associate cultivation of brilliance with either a particular "placement" or with sinus or nasal resonance. In English, Italian, and German, vowels and most consonants are oral-resonant, i.e., they are produced with the velum raised. However, it has often been asserted by singers and teachers of singing in the Western art tradition that resonance in the nasal passages and sinuses of the head plays an important part in tone production (Austin, 1995, 1997). Husler and Rodd-Marling (1976), for instance, claimed that different vocal functions are stimulated by different "placements" of the voice by which "the singer rouses (innervates) the inner and outer muscles of the throat" (p. 69). "Placing the tone in the forehead (often with the fictive idea of the sinuses as resonators)" (p. 71) is said to draw the larynx slightly upwards.

The chief result of what is often termed "singing in the mask", usually practised by placing the tone at the root of the nose, is to bring into action the main body of the muscle that lies in the vocal folds, the vocal *lip* (vocalis), i.e. the specific *Tensor*. (p. 70)

In 1987, Scotto di Carlo and Autesserre wrote:

To sing, one must necessarily lower the velum, or at least use velar positions as close to the lowered position as possible. (p. 7)

In speech, when the velum is raised to its highest point, it touches the rear pharyngeal wall, totally cutting off the nasal pharynx from the buccal cavity. This never occurs in singing where the nasal cavity always remains open, as we can see on the telexeroradiographic documents taken of various professional singers. (p. 12)

Troup, Welch, Volo, Tronconi, Ferrero, and Farnetani (1989) replied:

While not denying the validity of their research as applied to the group of singers studied, and to the language [French] sung by the subjects, we believe that velum closure in singing depends on many factors: the instructor, the language, the singer and the style of singing. (1989, p. 35)

In 1993, Alderson asserted:

directing a portion of the sound waves through the nasal cavity adds a more brilliant ring to the tone, while it is largely the responsibility of the oral cavity to turn sound waves into vowel colors. (p. 26)

Related to theories about the role of the nasal cavity in resonance are theories about the role of the sinuses, either as sound producers or sound modifiers. E. G. White's sinus tone theory of voice production maintains that voice is created in the skull sinuses. In addition, it emphasizes the role of the nasal cavity. According to this theory,

a well developed voice blends the activity of all the sinuses, variations in pitch and quality being determined by the extent to which the frontal sinuses are supplemented by the other cavities. In the highest notes the frontal sinuses, lying immediately above the eyebrow ridge, are predominant; they remain active throughout the compass but as the pitch is lowered vibrations spread more strongly to the ethmoid cells and sphenoid sinuses. Tone created in these sinuses is amplified in the larger volumes of air in the nasal cavity, the mouth, and the maxillary sinuses. (Hewlett, 1981, p. 13)

By contrast Wooldridge (1956), in a much-quoted study, compared the vowels produced by six professional singers under normal conditions and when the nasal passages had been filled with cotton gauze. A jury of expert listeners was unable to distinguish any difference. A repetition of the experiment by Vennard in 1964 (cited in Vennard, 1967) confirmed the original findings.

Austin (1997) compared the action of the velopharyngeal port in normal speech and Western operatic singers. He had four highly trained female singers read sentences containing nasal consonants at a normal conversational rate and then sing the sentences in recitative style in low, medium, and high singing ranges. For these singers, the velopharyngeal port was closed significantly longer in singing than in speaking. He found that the amount of time the velopyharyngeal port was opened was greatest in speech and diminished as the singer ascended in pitch.

Confusion about the role of the velum and the sinuses of the skull may stem from the singer's sensations of resonance, aural perceptions of "nasal resonance," and traditional exercises using the nasal continuants /m/, /n/, and /ŋ/. Miller (1993) attributed the confusion of "nasality with brilliance" to the "vocal tract adjustment that conducts sensations of balanced resonance to the bony and cartilaginous portions of the face, including the nasal cartilages, through sympathetic vibration" (p. 121). The "considerable controversy over whether vocal timbre, which is perceived by some singers and listeners as being marked by 'nasal resonance' but free of 'nasality', may also depend on laryngeal configuration as well as on internal vocal tract impedance" (Miller, 1986, p. 295).

For centuries, singers have used exercises based on /m/, /n/, and /ŋ/ for "improving resonance balance in vowels that follow them" (Miller, 1986, p. 80). The different nasals serve to stimulate different vibratory sensations in different areas. In /m/, for example,

> because the lips are closed, and because the mouth, pharynx, and the nostrils are now connected cavities, distinct vibratory sensations are felt in regions of the pharynx, the nose, the mouth, and the area of the sinuses. (Miller, 1986, p. 81)

In /n/ the vibrations are located higher, "in the region of the upper jaw and maxillary sinuses" (p. 89). In /ŋ/ "vibratory sensations in the frontal area of the face are often intense" (p. 85). Miller directed that in moving from the nasal to the vowel

> no continuance of actual nasality should be present in the tone, but the same *sensation* should pertain in the nasal and sinusal areas (sympathetic resonance experienced by the singer largely through bone and cartilage conduction). (p. 81)

Titze (1987) pointed out that confusion may arise when a singer's perception is linked to production without careful scrutiny of the acoustic signal. Different productions may lead to similar spectral patterns and hence similar perceptions. The ratio of the peak energy in the high-frequency portion of the spectrum (2 kHz to 4 kHz) to the peak energy in the low-frequency portion (0–1 kHz) is increased both when the singer's formant (brilliance) is produced, or when a vowel is nasalized. In the case of the singer's formant, the high-frequency prominence of the oral and pharyngeal resonance is increased by creating an additional resonator in the larynx. In the case of nasalization, the low-frequency prominence of the oral and pharyngeal resonance is lowered by creating an acoustic leakage through the nose. Lowering the velum and coupling the nasal cavity to the rest of the vocal tract introduces anti-resonances into the formant envelope. Nasalization reduces the intensity at and near the frequency of any of a number of anti-resonances, including between 2 and 3 kHz, the range in which the singer's formant occurs (Austin, 1995).

The difference between brilliance and nasality was clarified by a study conducted by Yanagisawa, Kmucha, and Estill (1990). By means of simultaneous velolaryngeal videoendoscopy, the study examined the role of the soft palate in normal laryngeal functions, as well as in its contribution to nasal and oral voice qualities. Singers executed a five-part task, beginning with a totally nasalized /ŋ/ and progressing to a nasalized /i/, a nasalized /i/ in twang quality, an oral /i/ in twang quality, and an /i/ in which the oral twang quality was modified by lowering the larynx. The sequential changes in quality were noted, from a completely nasal to a rather loud oral tone. The endoscopy verified that the first three conditions were indeed nasal, as judged by an open velopharyngeal port, while in the last two conditions, in which the velopharyngeal port was closed, the qualities were oral. The authors contrasted the dull quality, produced by nasality, with the bright quality of twang, produced by aryepiglottic constriction, qualities which have often been termed "nasal."

Experimental studies have thus clearly demonstrated that the production of brilliance in the voice is unrelated to the nasal passages or sinuses of the head.

## Vibrato

The vibrato used in Western classical singing is an undulation of the fundamental frequency. It seems that vibrato is produced by the phonatory mechanism rather than the respiratory mechanism (Cleveland, 1994). Vibrato can be described in terms of four parameters: the rate (number of undulations per second), the extent (how far phonation frequency departs up and down from its average during a vibrato cycle), the regularity (how similar the frequency excursions are to one another), and the waveform of the undulations (Sundberg, 1995b). Rate and extent are the two parameters most often studied.

Researchers have suggested that the periodic undulation of the fundamental frequency involved in vibrato may be a stabilized tremor of the cricothyroid and thyroarytenoid muscles (Titze, 1994; Hsiao, Solomon, Luschei, & Titze, 1994). How the stabilization is achieved is not yet certain. Many structures in the vocal tract, such as the velum, the tongue, and the side walls of the pharynx, may be engaged in a rhythmic pulsation synchronous with the vibrato; sometimes the tongue and lower jaw shake with the vibrator (Sundberg, 1987). Estill, Baer, Honda, and Harris (1984) found vibrato in the 5 to 6 Hz range in the suprahyoid muscles. Also, a natural resonance in the breathing system occurs at about 6 Hz, which is almost identical to the normal vibrato rate (Sundberg, 1987).

Shipp, Leanderson, and Sundberg (1980) found a significantly slower vibrato rate in male singers than in female singers; vibrato rate was uninfluenced by vocal pitch or by vocal effort. However, skillful singers vary the pitch oscillation and rate of vibrato in response to artistic judgment informed by the musical style. Shipp, Leanderson, and Haglund (1983) suggested that the extent of the oscillation is monitored by the singer principally through the auditory pathways and the rate is principally a function of the autonomic nervous system's influence on the vibrato generator. The acceptable rate of vibrato in classical Western singing styles has changed this century, varying from 6 to 7 Hz early in the century, to the 5.5 Hz more common today (Shipp et al., 1980; Titze, 1994). The pitch modulation varies approximately one semitone (Shipp et al., 1980; Shipp, Sundberg, & Doherty, 1988).

In order for vibrato not to interfere with the melody, its extent needs to decrease when rapid pitch changes occur. A study by Michel and Myers (1991) found that vibrato width increased with increasing crescendo, but remained constant in decrescendo. The greatest vibrato width occurred at the middle frequencies. Baken and Orlikoff (1987) suggested that the regular pitch variation of vibrato disguises the pitch fluctuations produced by articulation. Some researchers have distinguished between "frequency vibrato," "amplitude vibrato," and "timbre vibrato," although it is likely that they have a common origin (Schutte & Miller, 1991). Schutte and Miller found that "amplitude vibrato" and "timbre vibrato" were largely the result of the shifting prominence of the various partials and formants as fundamental frequency modulated.

## Acoustic Characteristics and Perceptual Judgment

A valuable study by Ekholm, Papagiannis, and Chagnon (1998) identified perceptual criteria used by voice experts for the assessment of voice quality in classical singing and related them to objective measurements taken from acoustic analysis of the voice signal. This study is helpful to singing teachers (and to scientists) in linking perceptual features with acoustic features and, by implication, with physical coordinations.

Sixteen male singers—four counter-tenors, seven tenors, and five baritones—were recorded in a medium-sized concert hall singing an excerpt from Mozart's concert aria *Ch'io mi scordi di te* with piano accompaniment. Samples of vowels /a/, /i/, and /o/ demanding constant pitch and loudness in the singer's mid range were then extracted from the recordings and submitted to spectral analysis. A panel of seven expert voice teachers evaluated the 16 audiotaped performances in terms of the perceptual categories "appropriate vibrato," "resonance/ring," "color/warmth," and "clarity/focus". These criteria were 4 of 12 generally accepted perceptual criteria that had been established in a previous study (Wapnick & Eckholm, 1997).

The investigators identified the standard for vibrato in professional Western classical singing as an ever-present, smooth, and fairly even undulation of the fundamental frequency of about 5 to 7 cycles per second, with an average excursion from the average frequency of less than ±1 semitone. The singers all produced data within a "normal" range: for baritones a rate of 5.1 to 6.8 cycles per second and extent of 3.6 to 5.1 per cent; for tenors a rate of 5.1 to 6.4 cycles per second and extent of 4.3 to 8.0 per cent; and for counter-tenors a rate of 5.1 to 6.2 cycles per second and extent of 3.5 to 7.5 per cent. A delayed onset of vibrato or a lack of vibrato resulted in a low rating from the judges. Of the two counter-tenors who sang with vibrato, the judges gave a higher ranking to the singer having an average vibrato rate of 6.0 Hz (closer to the usual rate for female voices than for baritones) and extent of 3.5%. While the counter-tenor who ranked lower had the more regular vibrato of the two, his average vibrato rate was lower at 5.4 Hz and the extent was much higher at 7.5%. Of the two baritones ranked either first or second in all criteria, the sample segment ranked lower for appropriate vibrato had an amplitude modulation of approximately 90%, as compared to 22% for the other segment.

"Resonance/ring" was acoustically identified by presence of the singer's formant. It has been shown that the auditory system serves as a band of filters, with the critical band (that bandwidth at which subjective responses of listeners change abruptly) varying as a function of frequency (Lieberman & Blumstein, 1988). Following Bloothooft and Plomp (1986), who used two critical bands of hearing in their study of the sound level of the singer's formant in professional singing, Ekholm, Papagiannis, and Chagnon measured spectral energy distribution and the mean spectral amplitude in two one third octave frequency bands, one centered at 2540 Hz and the other at 3140 Hz. As would be expected, the singer's formant range was lower in baritones than in tenors. Results for counter-tenors were similar to that for baritones.

There was a strong correlation of the perceptual ratings for "resonance/ring" and mean amplitude of sound level within the lower band for baritones, and within the upper band for tenors. A baritone with most of the spectral energy in the singer's formant above 2800 Hz, the upper critical band of hearing in that range, received clearly lower "resonance/ring" ratings than other baritones. Not surprisingly, counter-tenors (singing in falsetto) received low ratings on this criterion. One counter-tenor, however, had a singer's formant comparable to that found in baritones and was rated consistently higher. Laryngoscopic examination of this singer revealed that the cartilaginous part of the vocal folds was notably longer than expected, effectively decreasing the length of the membranous vibrating vocal fold to a size expected in females.

Taken in conjunction with findings on the center frequency of the singer's formant in different voice types, the findings of this study on the perception of "ring" are significant for the teaching of singing. Voice classification is a subtle and complex matter, involving a number of parameters. I mentioned earlier in this chapter that formant analysis is one factor that could be used as a guide in voice classification; in Chapter 6 other factors are discussed. Given appropriate classification according to *passaggi*, range, and optimal tessitura, it then needs to be borne in mind that the perceptual qualities of the voice should align with expectations for that voice type. The center frequency of the singer's formant needs to be appropriate for the voice type: Tenors sound like tenors if the center frequency is around 2.8 kHz, baritones like baritones if it is around 2.7 kHz, and altos like altos if it is around 3.2 kHz. While an expert musical ear is invaluable, acoustic analysis and computer-assisted visual feedback can assist student and teacher in achieving the articulatory adjustments necessary to effect the appropriate changes in voice quality.

The perceptual quality of "color/warmth" is associated with a strengthening of the fundamental frequency, lower formant frequencies, and a less pronounced singer's formant. It is consistent with a voice production using a lowered larynx. This study found strong correlations between ratings for "color/warmth" and "appropriate vibrato" and a higher spectral energy in the singer's formant range. A high positive correlation with mean "vowel formant" frequency was observed in baritones, and a significant negative correlation was observed in counter-tenors and tenors. The "color/warmth" rating for baritones was higher than that for counter-tenors and tenors. These last two findings can presumably be attributed to register and vowel-modification factors in those voices singing at higher pitches.

The perceptual criterion "clarity/focus" relates to the degree of nonharmonic noise in the vocal tone. The judges rated vowel segments with elevated levels of nonharmonic spectral energy lower on this criterion. Two singers displayed subharmonic components in the spectrogram. "Clarity/focus" showed a significant positive correlation with vowel formant frequency.

This study clarified the attributes of good voice quality appropriate for Western classical singing. Such voice quality needs a balance of vibrato rate and extent, a low rate of amplitude vibrato, and a vibrato present throughout each note. It needs good vowel definition and the warmth of tone conferred by a lowered larynx, balanced by the "ring" of the singer's formant with its spectral location within the appropriate bandwidth for the voice classification. While intonation accuracy was not a perceptual criterion in this study, poor intonation negatively affected the perception of all other qualities.

## References

Alderson, A. (1993). Positioning the velum. *Journal of Research in Singing and Applied Vocal Pedagogy, XVI*(2), 25–32.

Austin, S. F. (1995). Nasal resonance—Dispelling the myth. *Australian Voice, 1,* 18–23.

Austin, S. (1997). Movement of the velum during speech and singing in classically trained singers. *Journal of Voice, 11*(2), 212–221.

Baken, R. J. (1991). An overview of laryngeal function for voice production. In R. T. Sataloff (Ed.), *Professional voice: The science and art of clinical care* (pp. 19–47). New York: Raven Press.

Baken, R. J., & Orlikoff, R. F. (1987). The effect of articulation on fundamental frequency in singers and speakers. *Journal of Voice, 1*(1), 68–76.

Bloothooft, G., & Plomp, R. (1984). Spectral analysis of sung vowels. I. Variation due to differences between vowels, singers, and modes of singing. *Journal of the Acoustical Society of America, 75*(4), 1259–1264.

Bloothooft, G., & Plomp, R. (1985). Spectral analysis of sung vowels. II. The effect of fundamental frequency on vowel spectra. *Journal of the Acoustical Society of America, 77*(4), 1580–1588.

Bloothooft, G., & Plomp, R. (1986). The sound level of the singer's formant in professional singing. *Journal of the Acoustic Society of America, 79*, 2028–2033.

Carlsson, G., & Sundberg, J. (1992). Formant frequency tuning in singing. *Journal of Voice, 6*(3), 256–260.

Cleveland, T. F. (1994). A clearer view of singing voice production: 25 years of progress. *Journal of Voice, 8*(1), 18–23.

Coffin, B. (1980). *Overtones of bel canto. The phonetic basis of artistic singing.* Metuchen, NJ: Scarecrow Press.

Coffin, B. (1987). *Coffin's sounds of singing. Principles and applications of vocal techniques with chromatic vowel chart* (B. Coffin, Ed.). Metuchen, NJ: Scarecrow Press.

Denes, P. B., & Pinson, E. N. (1993). *The speech chain. The physics and biology of spoken language* (2nd ed.). New York: Freeman.

Detweiler, R. F. (1994). An investigation of the laryngeal system as the resonance source of the singer's formant. *Journal of Voice, 8*(4), 303–313.

Dmitriev, L., & Kiselev, A. (1979). Relationship between the formant structure of different types of singing voices and the dimensions of supraglottic cavities. *Folia Phoniatrica, 31*, 238–241.

Ekholm, E., Papagiannis, G., & Chagnon, F. (1998). Relating objective measurements to expert evaluation of voice quality in Western classical singing: Critical perceptual parameters. *Journal of Voice, 12*(2), 182–196.

Estill, J., Baer, T., Honda, K., & Harris, K. S. (1984). The control of pitch and quality, Part I: An EMG study of supralaryngeal activity in six voice qualities. In V. L. Lawrence (Ed.), *Transcripts of the twelfth symposium, Care of the professional voice, 1983, Pt I* (pp. 86–91). New York: The Voice Foundation.

Gauffin, J., & Sundberg, J. (1989). Spectral correlates of glottal voice source waveform characteristics. *Journal of Speech and Hearing Research, 32*, 556–565.

Gottfried, T. L., & Chew, S. L. (1992). Intelligibility of vowels sung by a countertenor. *Journal of Research in Singing and Applied Vocal Pedagogy, XVI*(1), 13–28.

Hewlett, A. D. (1981). *Think afresh about the voice* (3rd ed.). London: Classical Music Consultants.

Howard, D. M., Lindsey, G. A., & Allen, B. (1990). Toward the quantification of vocal efficiency. *Journal of Voice, 4*(3), 205–212.

Hsiao, T. Y., Solomon, N. P., Luschei, E. S., & Titze, I. R. (1994). Modulation of fundamental frequency by laryngeal muscles during vibrato. *Journal of Voice, 8*(3), 224–229.

Husler, F., & Rodd-Marling, Y. (1976). *Singing. The physical nature of the vocal organ.* London: Hutchinson.

Johansson, C., Sundberg, J., & Wilbrand, H. (1992). X-ray study of articulation and formant frequencies in two female singers. *Journal of Research in Singing and Applied Vocal Pedagogy, 16*(1), 30–41.

Lieberman, P., & Blumstein, S. E. (1988). *Speech physiology, speech perception, and acoustic phonetics*. Cambridge, England: Cambridge University Press.

Lindestad, P.-Å., & Södersten, M. (1988). Laryngeal and pharyngeal behavior in countertenor and baritone singing—A videofiberscopic study. *Journal of Voice, 2*(2), 132–139.

Manén, L. (1987). *Bel canto. The teaching of the classical Italian song-schools, its decline and restoration*. Oxford, England: Oxford University Press.

Michel, J. F., & Myers, R. D. (1991). The effects of crescendo on vocal vibrato. *Journal of Voice, 5*(4), 292–298.

Miller, D. G., & Schutte, H. K. (1990). Formant tuning in a professional baritone. *Journal of Voice, 4*(3), 231–237.

Miller, R. (1986). *The structure of singing. System and art in vocal technique*. New York: Schirmer Books.

Miller, R. (1993). *Training tenor voices*. New York: Schirmer Books.

O'Connor, J. D. (1973). *Phonetics*. Harmondsworth, Middlesex, England: Penguin.

Pickett, J. M. (1980). *The sounds of speech communication*. Baltimore: University Park Press.

Reid, C. L. (1990). The nature of resonance. *Journal of Research in Singing and Applied Vocal Pedagogy, 14*(1), 1–25.

Rothenberg, M. (1984). Source-tract acoustic interaction and voice quality. In V. L. Lawrence (Ed.), *Transcripts of the twelfth symposium, Care of the professional voice, 1983, Pt I* (pp. 25–31). New York: The Voice Foundation.

Schutte, H. K., & Miller, D. G. (1991). Acoustic details of vibrato cycle in tenor high notes. *Journal of Voice, 5*(3), 217–223.

Scotto di Carlo, N., & Autesserre, D. (1987). Movements of the velum in singing. *Journal of Research in Singing and Applied Vocal Pedagogy, XI*(1), 3–13.

Scotto di Carlo, N., & Rutherford, A. (1990). The effect of pitch on the perception of a coloratura soprano's vocalic system. *Journal of Research in Singing and Applied Vocal Pedagogy, XIII*(2), 11–23.

Sengupta, R. (1990). Study on some aspects of the "singer's formant" in North Indian classical singing. *Journal of Voice, 4*(2), 129–134.

Shipp, T., & Izdebski, K. (1975). Vocal frequency and vertical larynx positioning by singers and nonsingers. *Journal of the Acoustical Society of America, 58*(5), 1104–1106.

Shipp, T., Leanderson, R., & Haglund, S. (1983). Contribution of the cricothyroid muscle to vocal vibrato. In V. L. Lawrence (Ed.), *Transcripts of the eleventh symposium on care of the professional voice, 1982*, (pp. 131–133). New York: The Voice Foundation.

Shipp, T., Leanderson, R., & Sundberg, J. S. (1980). Some acoustic characteristics of vocal vibrato. *Journal of Research in Singing, 4*, 18–25.

Shipp, T., Sundberg, J., & Doherty, E. T. (1988). The effect of delayed auditory feedback on vocal vibrato. *Journal of Voice, 2*(3), 195–199.

Simonson, D. R. (1987). The relationship between the fundamental pitch, the first vowel formant and the singing formant: An acoustical experiment. Unpublished doctoral dissertation, Northwestern University, Evanston, IL.

Smith, L. A., & Scott, B. L. (1992). Increasing the intelligibility of sung vowels. *Journal of Research in Singing and Applied Vocal Pedagogy, XV*(2), 13–18.

Sundberg, J. (1974). Articulatory interpretation of the "singing formant". *Journal of the Acoustical Society of America, 55,* 838–844.

Sundberg, J. (1975). Formant technique in a professional female singer. *Acustica, XXXII*(2), 89–96.

Sundberg, J. (1977). The acoustics of the singing voice. *Scientific American, 236*(3), 82–91.

Sundberg, J. (Ed.) (1981). *Research aspects on singing.* Stockholm: The Royal Swedish Academy of Music.

Sundberg, J. (1983). Raised and lowered larynx: The effect on vowel formant frequencies. *Journal of Research in Singing, 6,* 7–15.

Sundberg, J. (1987). *The science of singing.* Dekalb, IL: Northern Illinois University Press.

Sundberg, J. (1991a). Vocal tract resonance. In R. T. Sataloff (Ed.), *Professional voice. The science and art of clinical care* (pp. 49–68). New York: Raven Press.

Sundberg, J. (1991b). Comparisons of pharynx, source, formant and pressure characteristics in operatic and musical theatre singing. *Speech Transmission Laboratory Quarterly Progress Status Report* (KTH, Stockholm), 2–3, 51–62.

Sundberg, J. (1995a). The singer's formant revisited. *Voice, 4,* 106–109.

Sundberg, J. (1995b). Acoustic and psychoacoustic aspects of vocal vibrato. In P. Dejonckere, M. Hirano, & J. Sundberg (Eds.), *Vibrato* (pp. 35–62). San Diego, CA: Singular Publishing Group.

Sundberg, J., & Skoog, J. (1996). Dependence of jaw opening on pitch and vowel in singers. *Journal of Voice, 11*(3), 301–306.

Teie, E. W. (1976). A comparative study of the development of the third formant in trained and untrained voices. Unpublished doctoral dissertation, University of Minnesota, Minneapolis, MN.

Titze, I. R. (1984). Rules for modifying vowels. *The NATS Bulletin, 40*(3), 30–31.

Titze, I. R. (1986). Voice research: Voice qualities governed by the velum and the epiglottis. *The NATS Journal, 42*(3), 24–25.

Titze, I. R. (1987). Voice research: Nasality in vowels. *The NATS Journal, 34*(4), 34–35, 37.

Titze, I. R. (1991). Voice research: Relations between acoustic power, intensity, loudness, and sound pressure level. *The NATS Journal, 47*(3), p. 31.

Titze, I. R. (1994). *Principles of voice production.* Englewood Cliffs, NJ: Prentice Hall.

Titze, I. R. (1995). Voice research: Speaking vowels versus singing vowels. *Journal of Singing, 52*(1), pp. 41–42.

Titze, I. R. (1997). Voice research: Are the corner vowels like primary colors? *Journal of Singing, 54*(2), pp. 35–38.

Titze, I. R. (1998). Voice research: The wide pharynx. *Journal of Singing, 55*(1), pp. 27–28.

Titze, I. R., & Story, B. (1977). Acoustic interactions of the voice source with the lower vocal tract. *Journal of the Acoustical Society of America, 101*(4), pp. 2234–2243.

Troup, G. J., Welch, G., Volo, M., Tronconi, A., Ferrero, F., & Farnetani, E. (1989). On velum opening in singing. *Journal of Research in Singing and Applied Vocal Pedagogy, XII*(1), 35–39.

Vennard, W. (1967). *Singing—the mechanism and the technic* (rev. ed.). New York: Carl Fischer.

Wang, S-q. (1985). The relationship between bright timbre, singer's formants and larynx position. *The NATS Bulletin, 41*(3), 20–22.

Wapnick, J., & Eckholm, E. (1997). Expert consensus in solo voice performance evaluation. *Journal of Voice, 11*(4), p. 429.

Wooldridge, W. B. (1956). Is there nasal resonance? *The NATS Bulletin, 13*(1), 28–29.

Yanagisawa, E., Estill, J., Kmucha, S. T., & Leder, S. B. (1989). The contribution of aryepiglottic constriction to "ringing" voice quality—a videolaryngoscopic study with acoustic analysis. *Journal of Voice, 4*, 342–350.

Yanagisawa, E., Kmucha, S. T., & Estill, J. (1990). Role of the soft palate in laryngeal functions and selected voice qualities. Simultaneous velolaryngeal videoendoscopy. *Annals of Otology, Rhinology and Laryngology, 99*, 18–28.

# C H A P T E R

## 6

# *Registration*

S inging teachers are interested in vocal registers in order to facilitate use of the whole range of the voice. Skill in negotiating register transitions also offers the ability to sing a gradually modulating quality through that range, avoiding sudden "breaks" in quality and loudness if that is aesthetically appropriate. McKinney identified registration as an area of vocal instruction "shrouded with mystery, semantic confusion, and controversy" (1982, p. 97). Over centuries there has been debate about whether vocal registers exist in the well-produced voice or whether they are evidence of a vocal fault, and if registers do exist, how many there are, what terms should be used for them, and at which pitches the transitions between registers occur (see, for example, McKinney, 1982; Doscher, 1994; Bunch, 1995; David, 1995).

The term "register" refers to a range of pitch having a consistent timbre. It is probably borrowed from the terminology of organ registration, referring to perceptually distinct regions of sound quality. In singing, the concept of register is concerned mainly with a change in voice quality at particular pitches due to changes in the action of the interdependent cricothyroid and the lateral and vocalis muscles of the larynx. Register transitions are more identifiable than registers themselves. Although vocal registers are commonly conceptualized as being regions of relatively constant quality in which pitch, loudness, and vowel can be adjusted somewhat at will, the identification of one register without reference to adjacent registers is difficult. Registers become more distinct as transitions become more abrupt (Titze, 1983).

The subject of vocal registers is controversial. Despite occasional minority support for a one-register or no-register position (see, for example, Lehmann, 1902/1952; Johnson, 1982), there is broad agreement among voice scientists, phoneticians, and voice teachers that registers do exist. There is, however, disagreement on the number of registers normal in the singing voice, the names given to them, the physiological factors involved, the pitches at which register changes occur, and how the teacher should deal with register changes to teach control of quality and intensity. There is disagreement not only across voice professions but also among singing teachers on the theory of register events and incorporation of this theory into an overall pedagogy.

## Register Terminology

One of the most vexed areas in regard to registers is the different terminologies employed by scientists, voice pathologists, spoken voice teachers, and singing teachers. Mörner, Fransesson, and Fant (1964) list 107 different names that have been used to identify registers. Each group conceptualizes registers in terms of its particular professional paradigm, adversely affecting interdisciplinary communication. As with many other areas of vocal terminology, performers and teachers of performers tend to use terms based on perception and body sensation, while scientists use terms related to observable, measurable physical phenomena. Much confusion arises from the fact that registration relates to a complex of factors concerned with pitch and timbre. McKinney (1982) ascribed the confusion to the use of the term "register" to describe many different things: 1. a particular part of the vocal range, 2. a resonance area, 3. a phonatory process, 4. a certain timbre, and 5. a region of the voice that is defined or delimited by vocal breaks.

Even among singing teachers there is substantial variation in register terminology. Timberlake's (1990) discussion of "terminological turmoil" presented a table of terms used since the 13th century. At that time singing—or at least the church and secular art singing that was the subject of theoretical writings—was a male preserve, and it continued to be dominated by men, including falsettists and castrati, into the 18th century. This century, male researchers and male subjects have dominated voice research. It is likely that these considerations have influenced the approach to registration.

The vocal range used by the repertoire of different periods is also a relevant factor. For example, the fact that Caccini (1602/1970) identified only two registers may relate to the limited range of his *"nuove musiche."* While the circumstances of performance and composition have changed greatly over the centuries, the same terms are current, often with changed meanings.

In 1981, the Collegium Medicorum Theatri (CoMeT) formed a committee of physicians, scientists, engineers, and voice pedagogues to review the position on vocal registers. In 1983, Hollien reported for CoMeT to the Voice Foundation's Twelfth Symposium, Care of the Professional Voice, stating that the committee had rejected the "old terms" and proposed using numbers to define the registers, as follows:

1. the very lowest register, probably used only in speaking (old terms: pulse, vocal fry, creak),
2. that (low) register, which is used for most speaking and singing (old terms: modal, chest, normal, heavy),
3. a high register used primarily in singing (old terms: falsetto, light, head)
4. a very high register usually found only in some women and children and not particularly relevant to singing (old terms: flute, whistle). (Hollien, 1984, p. 5; also referred to by Doscher, 1994)

The committee characterized the traditional terms "chest" and "head," which are based on the singer's sensation rather than on laryngeal mechanism, as "illogical if not absurd." These, and other traditional terms, are quite logical, however, in identifying either the kinesthetic or perceptual characteristic of a particular register—for example, the very lowest register is felt as a growl, perceived more as a pulse than as a continuous sound. But as a system of labeling, these terms have no internal consistency—for example, while "pulse" might be a logical perceptual term for the very lowest register, neither "modal" nor "heavy" seems a logical perceptual term for the next register. The term "chest register" is appropriate in light of recent scientific findings. Given that tracheal resonances carry energy into the upper thoracic region (Titze, 1985), there should be little objection to labeling the phenomenon according to the sensation identified by singers as characteristic of this register.

The CoMeT committee found it difficult to scientifically define the additional register in the middle of the frequency range (numbered 2A), but concluded that "it receives so much (subjective) support, it cannot be ignored" (Hollien, 1984, p. 5). The old terms identified for this register were "head," "mid," "middle," and "upper." It is this middle register which is of vital concern to singers and their teachers because it is in this area that most vocal repertoire lies. The committee was also comfortable with a heavy/light or lower/upper distinction.

## Definition of Registers

The classic 19th-century definition of singer/teacher/researcher Manuel Garcia is significant in linking the sound with the mechanism, the perceptual with the physiological:

> A register is a series of consecutive homogeneous sounds produced by one mechanism, differing essentially from another series of sounds equally homogeneous produced by another mechanism. (Garcia, 1894/1982, p. 8)

A complete operational definition of the phenomenon of vocal registration requires reference to perceptual, acoustic, physiological, and aerodynamic data. As yet, these data are far from complete. Schoenhard, Hollien, and Hicks (1984) maintained that singers' registers constitute entities that are different in many respects from speakers' registers. On the basis of data currently available on registers in the singing voice, it is clear that there are at least two laryngeally based registers (Hollien, 1974; Hirano, 1988). Some researchers have identified additional resonance-based (Hollien et al., 1976) or frequency-based (Titze, 1988) registers.

Leaving aside the extreme registers identified by the committee quoted above, two primary registers remain. Both of these registers seem to be determined largely by laryngeal function, and the "middle" register—of a range of an octave to a tenth—by a smooth transition, or overlap, between those two. Vennard's (1967) terminology for the two main registers has gained some acceptance; he used "heavy mechanism" and "light mechanism," referring to laryngeal function. Miller (1986) prefered the traditional Italian terms *"voce di petto"* and *"voce di testa,"* with the overlapping area called *"voce mista."* Many other writers and teachers use "chest," "middle," and "head." Referring to register events in terms of laryngeal function is logical and does imply other considerations, since the vocal folds react both to the subglottic air pressure and to the conformation of the supraglottic vocal tract. Many singing teachers subscribe to the realistic pedagogical approach of three registers, whatever the terminology used. Estill's teaching and research (1991, 1995, 1996a, 1996b) dealt with the problem in a logical way by referring to voice qualities defined in physiological, acoustic, and perceptual terms. For example, "speech quality" is defined as having: a neutral and relaxed vocal tract, with effort at

Flageolet Voice

oooh!
ahh!
arghh!

Flagellant Voice ....

COLINS

the larynx (physiology); a decreasing amplitude as frequency increases (acoustics); and the sound having "a certain presence" in the lower range and being easy to hear (perception) (Estill, 1995).

Some researchers have speculated on how women produce the high whistle register and whether it may rightly be regarded as a distinct register. It occurs above $F_6$ (1397 Hz), extending the pitch range of the coloratura soprano to the flageolet voice. Some have suggested that the sound is produced by air turbulence in the glottis, without significant vocal fold vibration (Titze, 1994). A study by Walker (1988) compared what the participants believed to be whistle register with what they believed to be head register. He found changes in spectra and airflow associated with an identifiable difference in voice quality, supporting the hypothesis that a change in source function is involved. What that change may be remains unclear.

## Register Change

Vocal register change is regulated mainly by the ratio of vocalis and cricothyroid activities (Hirano, 1988). If the ratio is changed abruptly, the register change is also abrupt and clearly heard. If the ratio is changed gradually, the register change is also gradual and less perceptible. If the change is also associated with a discontinuity of vocal fold vibrations, a "break" results. The mechanism of fundamental frequency control is different between the heavy or modal register and the light or falsetto register (Hirano, 1988). In the modal register, the activities of the cricothyroid, lateral cricoarytenoid, and vocalis are always positively related to fundamental frequency—that is, the activity increases with rising frequency and decreases with falling frequency. However, the vocalis muscle is antagonistic to the crico-thyroid in register control; if vocalis activity is not increased when cricothyroid activity increases to raise fundamental frequency, the balance between the two muscles will result in a shift to a lighter register. For the same register to be maintained, simultaneous increase in vocalis activity is necessary. In the light register, the activity of crico-thyroid, lateral cricoarytenoid, and vocalis is not always positively related to fundamental frequency. Hirano (1988) maintained that the cricothyroid, which plays the most important role in fundamental frequency control in the modal register, is not always active in the light register.

Schoenhard et al. (1984) made a perceptual study of registers in eight female singers. They found two perceptually recognizable registers that could also be differentiated on the basis of spectral contrasts. The "light register" exhibited more energy in the fundamental or first harmonic overtone; the "heavy register" exhibited more energy in the harmonic overtones above 5 kHz.

Keidar, Hurtig, and Titze (1987) also took a perceptual approach to identification of the primary registers, which they termed "chest" and "falsetto." Ten trained listeners were able to clearly perceive regis-ter boundaries and entities, with both male and female shift points identified at ~337 Hz and an average difference of less than two semi-tones between and within genders for different vowels. Listeners made discriminations more on the basis of quality than of pitch. Studies of vocal fry ("pulse register") have, however, found registers to be perceived primarily as a function of fundamental frequency (Keidar, 1986; Titze, 1988).

## Control of Registration

Abrupt changes in register may occur voluntarily or involuntarily. Titze (1988) suggested that involuntary timbre transitions result from resonances in the subglottal system (the trachea), and voluntary tim-bre transitions result from regulating vocal fold adduction. Transitions are less apparent in some voices than in others. If a voice is noticeably registered, a stair-step effect in quality is perceived. To avoid this, a singer should be able to change vocal quality continuously and gradu-ally over some significant range. Some teachers maintain that the voice exists only as a unity, and that if register changes exist, they are the result of poor technique rather than physiological factors. Good technique, however, rests on physiological efficiency, and if register changes are apparent in vocal production where aesthetic judgment determines they should not be, then the issue of vocal registers needs to be dealt with. Of course, the aesthetic judgment may be that an abrupt change in timbre is the right choice, as in yodeling, or sometimes in the large leaps used by composers for emotional effect. The singer needs to be able to choose, not to have the instrument dictate what happens.

A major issue in the study of registers is the consistency with which involuntary timbre transitions can be located at specific fundamental frequencies (Titze, 1988). For example, a major involuntary timbre transition is consistently found in the region of 300 to 350 Hz for both men and women. This *passaggio* seems to reflect the phenomenon of breaking into or out of the chest register. The transition can be smoothed out by training, as in the traditional approach to classical singing, or it can be accentuated and employed artistically as in yodeling, some country-western styles, and some contemporary classical repertoire.

There appear to be at least two ways in which timbre transitions can be executed voluntarily: (a) by changing adduction or (b) by changing lung pressure (Titze, 1988). An increase in lung pressure will increase the amplitude of vibration, thereby reducing the abduction quotient and enriching the timbre. The vocal processes would be spread apart slightly to offset the increasing amplitude of vibration as the pitch is raised. Alternatively, or additionally, the vocalis muscle could be relaxed gradually to allow the inferior part of the vocal fold to abduct. The adjustment could begin to take place somewhere around $C_4$, for example, and continue in varying amounts through $F_4$, with maximum equalization at $D_4$. If these mechanical factors are not finely coordinated, a change in timbre may be apparent.

A study by Roubeau, Chevrie-Muller, and Arabia-Guidet (1987) identified a succession of phenomena in the shift from one laryngeal mechanism to another in register change. First, there is an adjustment of the glottal configuration tied to variations in the tension of the muscles. This brings about a change in the shape of the glottal wave. This mechanical adaptation is followed by a reestablishment of a balance between the tensions of the vibrator and the subglottic pressure, which may occasion a temporary loss of control of fundamental frequency. Hill (1986) postulated that airflow is the critical factor in assisting register shift. Subglottic pressure and airflow increase as pitch increases, until the highest pitch of a given register is encountered. At this point, the mechanism shifts to a new and lower subglottic pressure and airflow. Increasing airflow over the *passaggio* facilitates the coordination of the two registers. Several researchers have also found that there is a time delay between the readjustment and stabilization of pitch in the new register (e.g., Roubeau, Chevrie-Muller, & Arabia, 1991).

At higher pitches, the singer needs both subglottal pressure increase and vowel modification to boost the output power and tune out the undesirable subglottal resonances. Supraglottal resonances, unlike the subglottal resonances, are highly adjustable by articulatory changes. Even within a given vowel category, the first and second formant frequencies can vary by as much as 50 to 100% (Titze, 1988). This makes formant tuning a sensible way to equalize timbre transitions resulting from subglottal resonances.

Studying the singing of octave displacements, MacCurtain and Welch (1985) found differences in vocal tract configurations between different registers as well as between bass and soprano singers. Both bass and soprano progressively widened the vocal tract in moving from "chest" to "head" register. While the basses tilted the larynx and lengthened the vocal tract in "head" register, the sopranos did neither. When the sopranos moved from "chest" (660 Hz) to "little" (1320 Hz), they narrowed and shortened the vocal tract. As discussed above, Lindestad and Södersten (1988) observed the same vocal tract configuration in countertenor singing at high pitch. These vocal tract gestures were not found in the baritone or bass in either study. Such gestures seems to cover the register transition by boosting the acoustic output through formant tuning.

In singing, the combination of rising pitch and high formant vowel results in an "open" or "white" quality. To counteract this tendency, front vowels may be modified in rising pitch so as to reduce the incidence of higher harmonic partials. Traditional pedagogies usually refer to this technique as vowel modification (Miller, 1986). "Covering" is another term used for this procedure, but since it is also used in other contexts it can be confusing (Miller, 1989).

Systematic vowel modification requires a knowledge of the phonetic categorization of vowels on the front-back/open-closed dimensions discussed above under resonance and articulation. Modification to an adjacent vowel (from back vowels to more central, from front vowels to more central, from closed vowels to more open) is employed at the *passaggio* as pitch rises. (See Miller's "Systematic Vowel Modification Chart," 1986, p. 157.)

Acoustically, this modification implies a change of formant frequencies and an elevated sound pressure level of the fundamental, resulting from an increased transglottal airflow. Hertegård, Gauffin, and Sundberg (1990) pointed out that "covered" singing near the *passaggio* shows similarities to flow phonation and is probably preferable from the point of view of vocal hygiene. Aesthetic judgments about word clarity and voice quality will affect the singer's decision about whether to use vowel modification, what type to use, and how much of it. Register equalization by adductory control is still an option.

The three factors involved in register control, identified both by scientific studies and writings on singing technique, are: subglottic air pressure, vocal fold adduction, and formant tuning. Many traditional pedagogies have advocated an approach based on one or more of these factors. For teachers, this means attention to the coordination between vocal fold adduction, breath management, and vocal tract conformation.

## Registration and Voice Classification

Much of the preceding discussion on breath management, phonation, and resonance makes clear that vowel formant frequency, vocal tract morphology, and subglottal pressure may all relate to voice type (Cleveland, 1977; Ågren & Sundberg, 1978; Dmitriev & Kiselev, 1979; Cleveland & Sundberg, 1985). Cleveland (1993a, 1993b) cited range, timbre, and tessitura as factors to be considered in classifying voices. The comfortable tessitura of the voice is related to register events, and teachers have often included the pitch at which register transitions occur as another factor to be considered.

Sundberg (1987) nominated the range of overlap between male "modal" and "falsetto" registers as in the vicinity of $G_3$ (200 Hz) to $F_4$ (350 Hz) but went on to state that "these ranges of register overlap, and the register boundaries vary substantially among individuals" (p. 51). Titze (1994), however, demonstrated that all investigators show a register transition between $D_4$ (294 Hz) and $G_4$ (392 Hz), spanning six voice categories. This major register transition represents the *primo passaggio* for females and *secondo passaggio* for males. Neither Sundberg (1987) nor Titze (1994) nominated particular pitches as register boundaries for the different voice types. Miller (1986), while not ruling out individual variation, did suggest $D_4$ (294 Hz) as the *passaggio* for bass, E-flat$_4$ for sopranos and dramatic baritones, $E_4$ for mezzo sopranos and dramatic tenors, and $G_4$ for lyric tenor, spinto tenor, and contralto. While it may not be possible to state with certainty the pitch at which a register shift will occur in a given voice, the general pattern across voice types is clear: The major shift occurs lowest in the bass and highest in tenor and contralto. This may serve as a guide for teachers in the classification of voices.

## References

Ågren, K., & Sundberg, J. (1978). An acoustic comparison of alto and tenor voices. *Journal of Research in Singing, 2*(1), 26–33.

Bunch, M. (1995). *Dynamics of the singing voice* (3rd ed.). Wien: Springer-Verlag.

Caccini, G. (1970). *Le nuove musiche* (H. Wiley Hitchcock, Ed.). Madison: A-R Editions. (Original work published 1602)

Cleveland, T. F. (1977). Acoustic properties of voice timbre types and their influence on voice classification. *Journal of the Acoustical Society of America, 61*(6), 1622–1629.

Cleveland, T. F. (1993a). Voice pedagogy for the twenty-first century: Toward a theory of voice classification (Part 1). *The NATS Journal, 49*(3), 30–31.

Cleveland, T. F. (1993b). Voice pedagogy for the twenty-first century: The importance of range and timbre in the determination of voice classification. *The NATS Journal, 49*(5), 30–31.

Cleveland, T. F., & Sundberg, J. (1985). Acoustic analysis of three male voices of different quality. In A. Askenfelt, S. Felicetti, E. Jansson, & J. Sundberg (Eds.), *Proceedings of Stockholm Music Acoustics Conference, 1983* (pp. 143–156). Stockholm: Royal Swedish Academy of Music.

David, M. (1995). *The new voice pedagogy.* Lanham, MD: Scarecrow Press.

Dmitriev, L., & Kiselev, A. (1979). Relationship between the formant structure of different types of singing voices and the dimensions of supraglottic cavities. *Folia phoniatrica, 31*, 238–241.

Doscher, B. (1994). *The functional unity of the singing voice* (2nd ed.). Metuchen, NJ: Scarecrow Press.

Estill, J. (1991). Compulsory figures for the master voice technician in speaking, acting, or singing. Unpublished course notes. Adelaide, Australia: Voice Craft.

Estill, J. (1995). *Voice craft. A user's guide to voice quality. Vol. 2: Some basic voice qualities.* Santa Rosa, CA: Estill Voice Training Systems.

Estill, J. (1996a). *Voice craft. A user's guide to voice quality. Level One: Primer of compulsory figures.* Santa Rosa, CA: Estill Voice Training Systems.

Estill, J. (1996b). Workshop: Compulsory figures for voice, 28 January to 2 February. Sydney, Australia: National Voice Centre.

Garcia, M. (1982). *Hints on singing* (rev. ed.) (Beata Garcia, Trans.). New York: Joseph Patelson Music House. (Original work published 1894)

Hertegård, S., Gauffin, J., & Sundberg, J. (1990). Open and covered singing as studied by means of fiberoptics, inverse filtering, and spectral analysis. *Journal of Voice, 4*(3), 220–230.

Hill, S. (1986). Characteristics of air-flow during changes in registration. *The NATS Journal, 43*(1), 16–17.

Hirano, M. (1988). The G. Paul Moore Lecture. Vocal mechanisms in singing: Laryngological and phoniatric aspects. *Journal of Voice, 1*(1), 51–69.

Hollien, H. (1974). On vocal registers. *Journal of Phonetics, 2*, 125–143.

Hollien, H. (1984). A review of vocal registers. In V. L. Lawrence (Ed.), *Transcripts of the twelfth symposium, Care of the professional voice, 1983, Pt I* (pp. 1–6). New York: The Voice Foundation.

Johnson, B. (1982). To have or have not—That is the question. In H. Hollien (Ed.), *Report on vocal registers*. New York: Collegium Medicorum Theatri.

Keidar, A. (1986). An acoustic-perceptual study of vocal fry using synthetic stimuli. *Journal of the Acoustical Society of America, 73*(Suppl 1), s. 3.

Keidar, A., Hurtig, R., & Titze, I. R. (1987). The perceptual nature of vocal register change. *Journal of Voice, 1*(3), 223–233.

Lehmann, L. (1952). *How to sing (Meine Gesangskunst)* (R. Aldrich, Trans.). New York: Macmillan. (Original work published 1902)

Lindestad, P.-Å., & Södersten, M. (1988). Laryngeal and pharyngeal behavior in countertenor and baritone singing—A videofiberscopic study. *Journal of Voice, 2*(2), 132–139.

MacCurtain, F., & Welch, G. (1985). Vocal tract gestures in soprano and bass: a xeroradiographic-electro-laryngographic study. In A. Askenfelt, S. Felicetti, E. Jansson, & J. Sundberg (Eds.), *Proceedings of the Stockholm Music Acoustics Conference, 1983, Vol. 1* (pp. 219–238). Stockholm: Royal Swedish Academy of Music.

McKinney, J. C. (1982). *The diagnosis & correction of vocal faults*. Nashville, TN: Broadman Press.

Miller, R. (1986). *The structure of singing. System and art in vocal technique*. New York: Schirmer Books.

Miller, R. (1989). Sotto voce: "Covering" in the singing voice. *The NATS Journal, 46*(2), 14–17.

Mörner, M., Fransesson, N., & Fant, G. (1964). Voice register terminology and standard pitch, *Speech Transmission Laboratory Quarterly Status Progress Report* (KTH, Stockholm), *4*, 12–15.

Roubeau, B., Chevrie-Muller, C., & Arabia, C. (1991). Control of laryngeal vibration in register change. In J. Gauffin, & B. Hammarberg (Eds.), *Vocal Fold Physiology* (pp. 279–286). San Diego, CA: Singular Publishing Group.

Roubeau, B., Chevrie-Muller, C., & Arabia-Guidet, C. (1987). Electroglottographic study of the changes of voice registers. *Folia phoniatrica, 39*, 280–289.

Schoenhard, C., Hollien, H., & Hicks, J. W., Jr. (1984). Spectral characteristics of voice registers in female singers. In V. L. Lawrence (Ed.), *Transcripts of the twelfth symposium, Care of the professional voice, 1983, Pt I* (pp. 7–10). New York: The Voice Foundation.

Sundberg, J. (1987). *The science of singing*. Dekalb, IL: Northern Illinois University Press.

Timberlake, C. (1990). Practica musicae: Terminological turmoil—The naming of registers. *The NATS Journal, 47*(1), 14–26.

Titze, I. R. (1983). Vocal registers. *The NATS Bulletin, 39*(4), 21–22.

Titze, I. R. (1985). The importance of vocal tract loading in maintaining vocal fold oscillation. In A. Askenfelt, S. Felicetti, E. Jansson, & J. Sundberg (Eds), *Proceedings of the Stockholm Music Acoustics Conference, 1983, Vol. 1* (pp. 61–72). Stockholm: Royal Swedish Academy of Music.

Titze, I. R. (1988). A framework for the study of vocal registers. *Journal of Voice, 2*(3), pp. 183–194.

Titze, I. R. (1994). *Principles of voice production.* Englewood Cliffs, NJ: Prentice Hall.

Vennard, W. (1967). *Singing—the mechanism and the technic* (rev. ed.). New York: Carl Fischer.

Walker, J. S. (1988). An investigation of the whistle register in the female voice. *Journal of Voice, 2*(2), 140–150.

# C H A P T E R

# 7

# *Vocal Health*

Recent publications on singing pedagogy make explicit what was in earlier works implicit in the whole approach to vocal technique: a concern for the maintenance of vocal health. Doscher (1994), Bunch (1995), and David (1995) all devoted sections to this subject. For all singers, a knowledge of how to care for the voice is necessary for the instrument to be available and in good condition whenever it is needed. For professional singers, keeping the voice in peak condition is necessary for earning a living, and yet the demands of busy schedules, demanding repertoire, and constant travel make that a difficult task.

Studies on vocal health for singers have produced prescriptions relating to maintaining hydration; managing general health, fitness, and lifestyle; avoiding vocal strain and fatigue; and using good technique to achieve efficient voice use.

## Hydration

Water is of extreme importance to the normal functioning of the respiratory tract and of the vocal tract in particular. Hydration is essential to the vocal folds because of the effects of friction. As the tissue vibrates, mechanical energy is dissipated into heat. The higher the frequency and the higher the intensity, the greater the friction. Loud high notes therefore pose particular problems. Well-irrigated vocal folds cope better with these problems, because they dissipate less energy (Titze, 1983b).

The greater part of the watery thin mucous manufactured by the nose is evaporated into the air that is breathed in through the nose. In this way, dry room air is moistened, and filtered, and warmed by the time it arrives at pharyngeal level. This fluid must be replaced, as must the fluid lost through exhalation and in the waste products of the body (Lawrence, 1986). Hydration requires particular attention in air-conditioned buildings or in the artificial atmosphere in airplane cabins, where usually the only humidity is produced by passengers exhaling moisture. Body hydration can be maintained by drinking copious amounts of water and by inhaling steam. Room atmosphere made dry by air-conditioning can be made humid by use of a humidifier. When the body is well hydrated, urine will be dilute, non-odorous, and clear.

### General Fitness, Health, and Lifestyle

For singers, the whole body is the instrument. Thus, the integrity and quality of the instrument are tied to the physiological and emotional well-being of the whole person (Holt & Holt, 1989). Singers require respiratory fitness, endurance, and general good health. Excess weight, lack of general condition, or failure to maintain good abdominal and thoracic muscle strength, all undermine the power source of the voice and predispose the singer to vocal difficulties (Sataloff, 1985). Dehydration, fatigue, and other general medical conditions may affect the mucosa covering the vocal folds, alter lubrication, and decrease vocal efficiency (Sataloff, 1986).

Good diet and sufficient sleep are an important part of maintaining general health and promoting vocal health and efficiency. Some singers find that the voice is adversely affected by certain foods such as dairy products, chocolate, and nuts (Sataloff, 1987a).

Dental problems or problems to do with the jaws may have harmful effects on the voice. Temporomandibular joint dysfunction, for example, introduces muscle tension in the head and neck, which is transmitted to the larynx directly through the muscular attachments between the mandible and the hyoid bone and indirectly as generalized increased muscle tension (Sataloff, 1987a). These problems may affect tongue movement and may also result in decreased range, vocal fatigue, and change in the quality or placement of the voice.

Any medical condition that interferes with efficient respiration and breath management may alter performance and cause voice abuse. When a singer complains to the laryngologist about changes in the voice, the problem is often not in the vocal folds, but rather in the production of adequate airflow. Minor alterations in respiratory function that would be barely noticed in the general population can have significant effects on a singer, causing vocal fatigue, loss of range, and hyperfunctional voice use (Spiegel, Sataloff, Cohn, & Hawkshaw, 1988). Alterations in respiratory function may be the result of asthma (most commonly), obstruction of the nasal airway, the pharynx or the larynx, and chest diseases (Spiegel, Sataloff, & Hawkshaw, 1990).

Allergies are becoming increasingly common, with many people reacting adversely to substances they inhale, ingest, or come into contact with. Allergic reactions may include upper respiratory problems (allergic rhinitis) and lower respiratory problems (asthma). Individuals may suffer seasonal allergic reactions or may be ill perennnially, depending on what causes their hypersensitivity (Sataloff, 1997). Unfortunately, singers may be sensitive to both the effects of their allergy and to the medications prescribed for it. They need to be referred to a medical specialist with a knowledge of voice.

In asthma, inflammation causes a narrowing of the airways and bronchospasm. This airway narrowing may be induced by the increased ventilation of exercise, including singing. Bronchospasm and airway narrowing plainly present problems to an artist relying on both stamina and subtlety in respiratory control. Physicians primarily direct treatment at reducing airway inflammation; therapy may also involve secondary treatment of bronchospasm. Because asthma can be life-threatening, asthmatic singers need treatment. From a vocal point of view, however, the cure may be worse than the complaint. The most common forms of asthma treatment involve long-term use of inhaled medication, which may affect the vocal folds and larynx. Inhaled corticosteroids seem to be particularly problematic for singers. Orally administered anti-inflammatory drugs and bronchodilator drugs are now available (Cohn, 1998). Allergy-directed therapy may also be appropriate. Plainly, asthmatic singers need to receive expert advice on the best management of their condition.

Conditions altering abdominal function, such as muscle spasm, constipation, or diarrhea, might be overlooked as a cause of vocal problems, but any condition interfering with efficient use of abdominal support may have deleterious effects on the voice (Sataloff, 1987a). Decrease in respiratory efficiency with aging may also affect the voice (Boone, 1993).

Singers need good medical advice on the prescription drugs that can be used to treat general medical problems without having an adverse effect on vocal function. Drugs may affect the voice by influencing proprioception and coordination, airflow, fluid balance, the

secretions of the upper respiratory tract, and the structure of the vocal folds (Martin, 1984). Many commonly used prescription drugs may have a harmful effect on the voice. Those with a dehydrating effect include antihistamines, diuretics, indigestion medications, sleeping pills, and some antibiotics (Holt & Holt, 1989; Lawrence, 1983; Sataloff, 1987a; Boone, 1993; Caputo Rosen & Sataloff, 1995). Large doses of vitamin C may also have a dehydrating effect (Lawrence, 1981). "Recreational" drugs, too, may adversely affect the voice. Alcohol, tobacco, and marijuana, for example, all have local irritant effects as well as blunting body sensation (Lawrence, 1983; Boone, 1993). Caffeine and alcohol, in addition, are dehydrating.

The voice is extremely sensitive to even slight hormone changes. Many of these are reflected as alterations of fluid content in the lamina propria of the vocal folds. This causes alteration in the mass and shape of the vocal folds and results in voice change, particularly muffling, sluggishness, decreased range, and loss of vocal efficiency (Sataloff, 1993). Hormonal changes in menopause, in menstruation, and in diseases such as hypothyroidism may cause such problems (Sataloff), as may changes induced by the use of drugs such as steroids, estrogen, and testosterone (Titze, 1994).

Voice problems related to sex hormones are seen most commonly in female singers. Vocal changes associated with the normal menstrual cycle have been the subject of a number of studies over the last

30 years (Brown & Hollien, 1984; Isenberger, Brown, & Rothman, 1984; Abitbol et al., 1989). While these changes have proven difficult to quantify, they are perceptually evident. Most ill effects are seen in the immediate premenstrual period in response to endocrine changes. These may include decreased vocal efficiency, loss of notes high in the range, vocal instability and fatigue, uncertainty of pitch, slight hoarseness, reduced vocal power and flexibility, and some muffling of the voice (Sataloff, 1993, 1996). While the effects of menopause have not been as widely studied, it is likely that the endocrine changes following menopause would have similar effects to those of the premenstrual phase (Sataloff, 1996). Pregnancy commonly results in voice changes similar to premenstrual symptoms (Sataloff, 1993). Birth control pills composed predominantly of estrogen seem not to affect the larynx, but those that are progestin-dominant may have a masculinizing or virilizing effect on the female larynx (Lawrence, 1983; Martin, 1988). Androgenic hormonal treatments are also used in the treatment of endometriosis, hormonal imbalances, and fibrocystic breast disease. Singers and their teachers need to be aware that when synthetic derivatives of testosterone are used, there is a risk of vocal fold changes, and in the case of long-term use, investigators have reported irreversible deepening of the voice (Martin, 1988).

Sataloff (1987b) suggested that steroids may be helpful for short-term use in treating cases of acute inflammatory laryngitis associated with oversinging, exposure to smoke, or the dehydrating effects of air travel.

Anything that affects sensory feedback may cause a loss of vocal control. Hearing loss interferes with auditory feedback and may result in altered vocal production, particularly if the singer is unaware of the hearing loss (Sataloff, 1987a). Even the common cold, when it affects internal hearing, may cause difficulties in vocal control (Lawrence, 1983). Medications that blunt sensation, such as throat sprays and lozenges containing topical anesthetics, tranquilizers, antidepressants, and some types of blood pressure medication, should be avoided if possible (Lawrence). Psychoactive medications need to be carefully monitored, since nearly all psychoactive medications have effects which can interfere with vocal tract physiology (Caputo Rosen & Sataloff, 1995).

Most voice disorders are related to tissue changes in the vocal fold cover (Titze, 1994). Changes may result from viral or bacterial infection (as in laryngitis associated with colds or influenza, or in bronchitis or croup) from irritation from pollutants in the atmosphere, or from smoking.

Aspirin is a drug that may affect vocal fold tissue. Commonly used alone for pain relief and also in combination with other drugs in many over-the-counter medications, aspirin (and other anti-inflammatories) may have a direct effect on blood coagulation by binding the calcium ion with which it comes in contact so that the calcium is not as immediately available for blood clotting. It also increases the fragility of capillaries, which may cause hemorrhage into the vocal folds in loud or high singing (Lawrence, 1983; Martin, 1984; Boone, 1993). Recovery from vocal fold hemorrhage usually requires at least two weeks voice rest (Lawrence).

Gastroesophageal reflux may also have an adverse effect on the vocal folds. Ross, Noordzji, and Woo (1998) found that 49 patients with suspected laryngopharyngeal reflux disease all showed significantly increased abnormal perceptual voice characteristics, which they termed musculoskeletal tension, hard glottal attack, glottal fry, restricted tone placement, and hoarseness. While gastroesophageal reflux may be caused by a hernia, it may also arise from the lifestyle of a performer (Lawrence, 1983; Sataloff, 1987a; Boone, 1993). Many singers avoid eating before a performance, eating the major meal of the day at night to relax after the performance, and then going straight to bed. Digestion then occurs with the body in a prone position, and gastric reflux may result. This may cause reddening and swelling of the vocal folds, with consequent hoarseness the next morning. Cleveland (1990) found a history of reflux and allergy in singers with intermittent pitch problems.

The eating disorder bulimia nervosa can cause a range of problems from edema through granulomas, nodules, polyps, and contact ulcers. Reflux may be a contributing factor to vocal disorders in singers with bulimia (Rothstein, 1998). Alterations in the mucosa of the larynx and pharynx similar to those found in reflux laryngopharyngitis have also been found in fungal infections such as candidiasis (Forrest & Weed, 1998).

### Vocal Strain and Fatigue

It is not known why vocal endurance is widely variable, with some singers able to endure prolonged voice use without risk while others succumb early to fatigue. Titze (1983a) postulated that vocal fatigue is linked to inefficient use of the mechanism, to muscular fatigue, and to dehydration. Fatigue may result when the mechanism is asked to perform a task requiring unaccustomed muscle use. Some muscle fatigue can be expected to occur after prolonged periods of phonation, regardless of how well the muscles are developed.

It is probable that vocal fatigue is physiologically similar to muscle fatigue in any other part of the body (Titze, 1983b). Vocal fatigue may result both from the fatiguing of respiratory and laryngeal muscles and from biomechanical changes in nonmuscular tissues that cause the vocal folds to vibrate less efficiently (Titze, 1983c). It is likely that many of the principles associated with muscle growth, maintenance, and deterioration in athletics may also apply to vocal performance.

The risk of vocal strain is minimized by warming up the voice before use and avoiding noisy environments that encourage overuse, such as singing over loud electric instruments, talking or singing in noisy nightclubs, and shouting at sporting events. Cooling down has long been advocated after extended athletic effort. While it is rarely mentioned in the vocal literature, it would seem a sensible procedure after extended vocal effort.

## Vocal Efficiency

Vocal efficiency in singing relies on both good health and good technique to supply energy and stamina and to regulate the fine changes in balance between respiratory and laryngeal function necessary to meet musical demands. Continuing vocal efficiency can be promoted by maintaining a regular practice schedule, by warming up before performance, by cultivating good speech habits, and by employing strategies to deal with the demands of performance. Optimum vocal conditioning requires following a specific regimen of daily vocalization to promote stamina in the respiratory system, coordination of voice onset and release, unification of the registers, resonance balancing, pitch, and dynamic control (Miller, 1986).

Sabol, Lee, and Stemple (1995) investigated the effects of isometric-isotonic vocal function exercises, practiced regularly for four weeks, on parameters of voice production in the healthy singer. Their 20 subjects were graduate-level voice majors of similar age and vocal training. They were divided into experimental and control groups, each containing three men and seven women. Each group continued their regular singing practice regimen, and the experimental group added the vocal function exercise program. Beginning from an assumption that exercise of the isometric type is not always an essential ingredient in singers' practice regimens, the researchers introduced the following exercises to be performed in the very soft part of the dynamic range:

1. Sustain /i/ as long as possible on a comfortable note ($F_4$).
2. Glide from the lowest to the highest note in the frequency range, using /o/.

3. Glide from the highest to the lowest note in the frequency range, using /o/.
4. Sustain the musical notes middle C and D, E, F, G above middle C for as long as possible, using /o/ (one octave lower for males). Repeat these notes two times. (p. 29)

At the end of the program, the experimental subjects showed significant positive changes in vocal function. They displayed significantly increased phonation volumes at all pitch levels, with a decreased flow rate. Maximum phonation times also improved. In other words, voice use became much more efficient.

This 1995 study displayed an interest in vocal efficiency and how to achieve it. Both the interest in vocal efficiency and the means used to achieve it are those advocated by traditional pedagogies over hundreds of years. Tosi, for example, writing in the 18th century, gave these directions to the student:

> Let him learn the Manner to glide with the Vowels and to drag the Voice gently from the high to the lower Notes, which, tho' Qualifications necessary for singing well, cannot possibly be learned from Sol-fa-ing only, and are overlooked by the Unskilful [sic]. (1743/1987, pp. 29–30)

It is likely that the success of the vocal function exercises used in the study was attributable not only to the type of exercises used, but also to the fact that a short sequence was repeated twice, done twice a day, every day of the week, with progress monitored three times a week. These conditions are ideal for the acquisition of a physical skill and closely model those adopted by the old Italian School. While participants were asked to list the vocal exercises they usually practiced, they were not asked to describe the duration or frequency of practice, nor how often it was monitored. These factors may be just as decisive, or even more decisive, in the positive result than the actual exercises performed.

In maintaining optimum vocal functioning, warming up before rehearsal and performance is necessary, as is avoiding fatigue by "marking" in lengthy production rehearsals. Titze (1993) suggested that vocal athletes need to adopt the warm-up principles of gymnasts, figure-skaters, and dancers, stretching joints, tendons, ligaments, and muscles. Glides over a large range of pitches and intensities constitute laryngeal and respiratory stretching exercises. Arpeggios, scales, and glissandos serve this purpose. As in developing any motor skill, exercises to increase accuracy of targeting, stability of posturing, speed of transitions, and dynamic range are advisable (Titze, 1993). Singers can practice the accuracy of pitch targeting by attacking notes at various pitches; the stability of posturing by singing long, sustained notes; and the speed of transition by executing rapid scales or arpeggios. Singers can extend range by executing quick leaps between high and low notes. Finally, singers can practice independence of phonation and articulation through consonant-vowel alterations, rapidly executed on scales or arpeggios. Having accessed the entire range of pitch and vocal quality, the singer should complete the warm-up with some loud singing.

Miller's (1990) prescription for a 20-minute warm-up procedure had much in common with that outlined above. He recommended that the singer begin with gentle, brief onsets and offsets in a comfortable range of the voice, progressing to humming in medium range and syllables with nasals and vowel sequences. Next the singer performs exercises for flexible tongue and jaw action, followed by agility patterns, both ascending and descending. Miller suggested a few minutes rest before turning to passages that deal with vowel definition and modification or with sostenuto. Registration and *passaggio* vocalises follow. Undertaking an established warm-up routine before performance offers psychological as well as physical security to the singer. Singing teachers and choral conductors should also use a warm-up routine before beginning work with the voice (Miller). Titze (1993) summarized the purpose of the warm-up as obtaining, as quickly as possible, a uniform vocal quality over a wide pitch range. Estill (1996b) recommended sirening up and down the range on /ŋ/, using "thin folds, a tilted thyroid and maximum effort, i.e., as hard a feeling of effort in the head with as soft a sound as possible in the larynx, without any break or roughness or change of quality either ascending or descending the scale" (1996a, p. 91) as the only warm-up necessary to achieve this.

Singers and singing teachers can underestimate the effect of the speaking voice on the singing voice. Misuse of the speaking voice, or use of a tired speaking voice, has direct and indirect effects on the singing voice. Teachers need to be alert to the risks posed by occupations such as teaching or aerobics instruction (Smith, Gray, Dove, Kirchner, & Heras, 1997; Smith, Kirchner, Taylor, Hoffman, & Lemke, 1998; Kostyk & Putnam Rochet, 1998; Long, Williford, Scharff Olson, & Wolfe, 1998). Direct effects are hoarseness and vocal fatigue. An indirect effect may be uncertainty about the reliability of the voice in singing, or even fear of singing (Cooper, 1982). Using the speaking voice at its optimal pitch is important to vocal health (Gregg, 1990; Titze, 1994). Boone (1977) suggested about 100 Hz (A-flat$_2$) as appropriate for basses, about 135 Hz (C#$_3$) for tenors, about 200 Hz (G#$_3$) for altos, and about 256 Hz (C$_4$) for sopranos. Researchers have identified speaking at too low a pitch as a significant factor in voice problems (Drew & Sapir, 1995).

While teachers of singing cannot be expected to have detailed knowledge of pathologies and medications, they do need to be sufficiently informed and aurally aware to distinguish between poor vocal technique and possible vocal damage. They need a knowledge of fitness and lifestyle management both to maintain their own vocal fitness in what has been identified as a high-risk profession and to advise their students on such issues. They also need to be in contact with a wider network of professionals in related fields—teachers of spoken voice; body use professionals such as Alexander, Feldenkrais and yoga teachers; dentists and orthodontists; otolaryngologists, speech therapists and voice care teams—with whom they can work and to whom students with vocal problems can be referred.

## References

Abitbol, J., de Brux, J., Millot, G., Masson, M.-F., Mimoun, O., Pau, H., & Abitbol, B. (1989). Does a hormonal vocal cord cycle exist in women? Study of vocal premenstrual syndrome in voice performers by videostroboscopy-glottography and cytology on 38 women. *Journal of Voice, 3*(2), 157–162.

Boone, D. R. (1977). *The voice and voice therapy.* Englewood Cliffs, NJ: Prentice-Hall.

Boone, D. R. (1993). Biologic enemies of the professional voice. *Journal of Research in Singing and Applied Vocal Pedagogy, 16*(2), 15–24.

Brown, W. S. & Hollien, H. (1984). Effects of menstruation on the singing voice. In V.L. Lawrence (Ed.), *Transcripts of the twelfth symposium, Care of the professional voice, 1983, Pt I* (pp. 112–116). New York: The Voice Foundation.

Bunch, M. (1995). *Dynamics of the singing voice* (3rd ed.). Wien: Springer-Verlag.

Caputo Rosen, D. & Sataloff, R. T. (1995). Laryngoscope: Psychoactive medications and their effects on the voice. *The NATS Journal, 52*(2), 49–53.

Cleveland, T. F. (1990). Vocal pedagogy in the twenty-first century: Some new observations on pitch problems. *The NATS Journal, 46*(3), 34–35, 52.

Cohn, J. (1998). Laryngoscope: Asthma and the serious singer. *Journal of Singing, 54*(3), 51–53.

Cooper, M. (1982). The tired speaking voice and the negative effect on the singing voice. *The NATS Bulletin, 39*(2), 11–14.

David, M. (1995). *The new voice pedagogy.* Lanham, MD: Scarecrow Press.

Doscher, B. (1994). *The functional unity of the singing voice* (2nd ed.). Metuchen, NJ: Scarecrow Press.

Drew, R., & Sapir, S. (1995). Average speaking fundamental frequency in soprano singers with and without symptoms of vocal attrition. *Journal of Voice, 9*(2), 134–141.

Estill, J. (1996a). *Voice craft. A user's guide to voice quality. Level One: Primer of compulsory figures.* Santa Rosa, CA: Estill Voice Training Systems.

Estill, J. (1996b). Workshop: Compulsory figures for voice, 28 January to 2 February. Sydney, Australia: National Voice Centre.

Forrest, L., & Weed, H. (1998). Candida laryngitis appearing as leukoplakia and GERD. *Journal of Voice, 12*(2), 91–95.

Gregg, J. W. (1990). From song to speech: On pitch. *The NATS Journal, 46*(3), 37, 50, 52.

Holt, G. A., & Holt, K. E. (1989). Laryngoscope: Medications—Aids to singing health? *The NATS Journal, 45*(4), 21–24.

Isenberger, H., Brown, W. S., & Rothman, H. (1984). Effects of menstruation on the singing voice. Part II: Further developments in research. In V. L. Lawrence (Ed.), *Transcripts of the twelfth symposium, Care of the professional voice, 1983, Pt I* (pp. 117–123). New York: The Voice Foundation.

Kostyk, B. E., & Putnam Rochet, A. (1998). Laryngeal airway resistance in teachers with vocal fatigue: A preliminary study. *Journal of Voice, 12*(3), 287–299.

Lawrence, V. L. (1981). Laryngoscope: Vitamin C. *The NATS Journal, 37*(5), 24–25.

Lawrence, V. L. (1983). Laryngoscope: When all else fails, read the instructions. *The NATS Journal, 39*(3), 16–19.

Lawrence, V. L. (1986). Laryngoscope: Marijuana and cocaine. *The NATS Journal, 43*(2), 26–27.

Long, J., Williford, H. N., Scharff Olson, M., & Wolfe, V. (1998). Voice problems and risk factors among aerobics instructors. *Journal of Voice, 12*(2), 197–207.

Martin, F. G. (1988). Drugs and vocal function. *Journal of Voice, 2*, 338–344.

Martin, F. G. (1984). Drugs and the voice. In V. L. Lawrence (Ed.), *Transcripts of the twelfth symposium, Care of the professional voice, 1983, Pt I* (pp. 124–132). New York: The Voice Foundation.

Miller, R. (1986). *The structure of singing. System and art in vocal technique.* New York: Schirmer Books.

Miller, R. (1990). Sotto voce: Warming up the voice. *The NATS Journal, 46*(5), 22–23.

Ross, J-A., Noordzji, J., & Woo, P. (1998). Voice disorders in patients with suspected laryngo-pharyngeal reflux disease. *Journal of Voice, 12*(1), 84–88.

Rothstein, S. (1998). Reflux and vocal disorders in singers with bulimia. *Journal of Voice, 12*(1), 89–90.

Sabol, J. W., Lee, L., & Stemple, J. C. (1995). The value of vocal function exercises in the practice regimen of singers. *Journal of Voice, 9*(1), 27–36.

Sataloff, R. T. (1985). Laryngoscope: Ten good ways to abuse your voice: A singer's guide to a short career (Part 1). *The NATS Journal, 42*(1), 23–25.

Sataloff, R. T. (1986). Laryngoscope: Voice rest. *The NATS Bulletin, 43*(5), 23–25.

Sataloff, R. T. (1987a). The professional voice: Part I. Anatomy, function, and general health. *Journal of Voice, 1*(1), 92–104.

Sataloff, R. T. (1987b). Laryngoscope: A "first aid kit" for singers, *The NATS Journal, 43*(4), 26–29.

Sataloff, R. T. (1993). Laryngoscope: Hormones and the voice. *The NATS Journal, 50*(1), 43–45.

Sataloff, R. T. (1996). The effects of menopause on the singing voice. *Journal of Singing, 52*(4), 39–42.

Sataloff, R. T. (1997). Laryngoscope: Allergy. *Journal of Singing, 53*(4), 39–43.

Smith, E., Gray, S. D., Dove, H., Kirchner, L. & Heras, H. (1997). Frequency and effects of teachers' voice problems. *Journal of Voice, 11*(1), 81–87.

Smith, E., Kirchner, H. L., Taylor, M., Hoffman, H. & Lemke, J. H. (1998). Voice problems among teachers: Differences by gender and teaching characteristics. *Journal of Voice, 12*(3), 328–334.

Spiegel, J. R., Sataloff, R. T., Cohn, J. R., & Hawkshaw, M. (1988). Respiratory function in singers: Medical assessment, diagnoses, and treatments. *Journal of Voice, 2*(1), 40–50.

Spiegel, J. R., Sataloff, R. T., & Hawkshaw, M. J. (1990). Laryngoscope: Respiratory function and dysfunction in singers. *The NATS Journal, 46*(4), 23–25.

Titze, I. R. (1983a). Vocal fatigue. *The NATS Bulletin, 39*(3), 22–23.

Titze, I. R. (1983b). A further look at vocal fatigue: Part I. *The NATS Bulletin, 40*(1), 33–34

Titze, I. R. (1983c). A further look at vocal fatigue: Part II. *The NATS Bulletin, 40*(2), 29–30.

Titze, I. R. (1993). Voice research: Warm-up exercises. *The NATS Journal, 49*(5), p. 21.

Titze, I. R. (1994). *Principles of voice production.* Englewood Cliffs, NJ: Prentice Hall.

Tosi, P. F. (1987). *Observations on the florid song* (Galliard, Trans., M. Pilkington, Ed.). London: Stainer & Bell. (Original work published in 1943.)

# CHAPTER

# 8

# *Teaching Singing*

*... feeling is an inseparable part of everything
that happens in the conscious life of the psycho-
physical organism. One of the most important
aspects of this is the relation of feeling to cognition.*
*(Reid, 1986, p. 18)*

*Research neither destroys the magic of music nor
trivialises educational transactions.*
*(Swanwick, 1994, p. 71)*

## What Scientists Know About Singing

It is difficult to draw firm conclusions about the implications for
singing pedagogy of many scientific studies. The utility of experimental findings for the teaching of singing depends on their incorporation
into a theory of the singing voice and on their relation to current
practice. Apart from this, other difficulties arise from researchers
neglecting experimental detail that is important from the singing
teacher's point of view.

One difficulty is that much of the experimental work exists as
studies of discrete aspects of voice using a small number of subjects.
In some cases, it is difficult to identify what pedagogical tradition the
singers represent and to link the vocal strategies used with a perceptual result. Generalizing from such studies is difficult.

A second difficulty is that in many studies, singers produce only isolated syllables or sustained vowels, or they may sing in only a limited pitch range. It is then unclear what conclusions may be made about singing connected phrases over a wider pitch range.

A third difficulty relates to sample populations. While in the last 10 years or so it has become more common to give details of subjects' voice type, years of training, and singing experience, many studies still compare amateur singers with postgraduate students and retired professionals. It is then difficult to generalize from the findings. A similar consideration is that studies often do not distinguish between different categories of voice belonging to the same general voice type (e.g., between a lyric tenor and a *Heldentenor*, or between a coloratura soprano and a spinto soprano). Nor, in most cases, do they distinguish between different voice types (e.g., a baritone and a bass-baritone). In some studies, "a singer is a singer is a singer" and "a baritone is a baritone is a baritone." This is unfortunate, because such categorization may well be relevant to register, range, voice quality, or flexibility and have a significant impact on results.

A fourth difficulty is that most studies say nothing about how much preparation or warm-up was done by the subjects. Nor, when invasive experimental techniques are used, is it clear how these techniques may have affected participants' performances.

A fifth difficulty is that it is not clear from most studies what consequences different vocal strategies might have for vocal sound or for vocal control. For example, do "belly-in" and "belly-out" strategies of breath management produce any difference in sound quality? What is their comparative effectiveness in relation to sustained singing in different pitch ranges, to executing leaps, or to singing coloratura passages?

Perhaps the most important difficulty in interpreting results of experimental investigations is the fact that male and female voices differ in many respects. Historically, most investigators have been men, as have most subjects (often the experimenters or their colleagues). This has led to construction of a model of the singing voice that is essentially a model of the *male* voice. So many instances have accumulated in which the female voice represents a deviation from this model that it is time to rethink the model. Titze (1994) advocated use of the adult female voice as a standard because for women, vocal physiology represents a strong connection with units of the metric system. For example, the vibrating vocal fold length is of the order of 1 cm; the vibration amplitude is of the order of 1 mm; the mass of a vocal fold is of the order of 1 g; the maximum aerodynamic power in phonation is of the order of 1 W, and so on. Another solution would be to devise a much more complex and sophisticated model, based on extensive work with all types of voices, to replace the inadequate gender-based model in use at present.

Nevertheless, with respect to some aspects of vocal functioning, results from an accumulation of studies allow generalization. Some important findings can be identified.

In relation to respiration, basic research has provided insight into optimal methods of inspiration, relative posturing of the chest and abdomen, and muscular control of expiration. Because the respiratory mechanism provides the airflow and subglottic pressure for singing, phonatory problems often have their origin in either airflow or sub-glottic pressure, or in the fine balance between the two necessary for laryngeal efficiency. An important finding is that flow phonation, resulting from less adductory force of the vocal folds and more air-flow, allows production of vocal intensity with economical breath use and places less mechanical stress on the vocal folds.

Research has not yet, however, determined what is involved in "support" of the voice. Because control of subglottal pressure relies on a complex system of passive recoil forces and active muscular forces to achieve an ideal operation of the thoracic, diaphragmatic, and abdominal aspects of respiration, there is no simple formula for support. It is more likely that control of respiration for singing needs to be a dynamic coordination related to body type and specific musical demands.

While the area of vocal registration still presents problems of definition and terminology, the pitch range within which the major register change occurs has been identified. Control of involuntary timbre transitions can be achieved through coordination of subglottic air pressure, laryngeal operation, and formant tuning. With the benefit of instrumental acoustic analysis, it is now possible to be quite specific about the effect of particular articulatory maneuvers on vocal resonance for this purpose, for the production of the singer's formant, and for control of vocal timbre. Voice classification may be assisted by data on the frequencies at which register changes and the singer's formant occur in the different voice types.

Experimental research on the relation between airflow, laryngeal operation, and vocal tract resonances confirms the traditional wisdom that singers should adopt strategies that decouple the articulatory and phonatory systems. Such strategies contribute to control of fundamental frequency while maintaining the vibrancy of the voice.

In the area of physical efficiency and vocal health, there is a body of voice science knowledge readily available to practitioners. Findings on the utility of visual feedback from instrumentation are also of immediate applicability in the teaching of vocal skills in the studio setting.

## What Singing Teachers Know About Voice

The vocal instrument is unlike any other musical instrument in that much of it cannot normally be seen, and its workings cannot normally be observed. For hundreds of years, therefore, teachers of singing, unlike teachers of any other musical instrument, have practiced their profession without any detailed knowledge of how the vocal instrument works. In the absence of such knowledge, teachers have relied on their informed auditory discrimination, their musical judgment, the extensive body of practical knowledge developed by the profession, and their own experience of singing. Teaching has been a matter of demonstrating and describing what has to be achieved and what sensations are felt in achieving it, and thus conveying experiential knowledge—the soma of singing—to students.

What most singing teachers know about voice, then, is based on use of the whole body as a musical instrument. They are concerned about body alignment and use, the mental skills of audiation, and fine control of vocal tone. They strive to develop these qualities in their students through general music education, informed listening, and observation of master singers.

Beginning singing teachers are usually much older than beginning voice scientists. While many singers teach a little to supplement their income, those who devote themselves to teaching usually do so after some kind of career as a singer. There are probably three reasons for this: first, performing is valued above teaching; second, teachers feel an obligation to have experienced the demands of performance and to have a wide knowledge of music, of vocal repertoire, and of the languages used in the standard repertoire before embarking on a teaching career; and, third, many retired singers are still eager to work and naturally turn to teaching as a way of using their professional skills and continuing to contribute to the world of singing.

Teachers are aware that singing is an intensely personal experience, involving the whole person—mind, body, emotions. They also are mindful of the need to understand and communicate with a range of personalities, to facilitate development of a range of intellects, and to provide support to singers in what can be a testing professional environment. They know that anything that threatens physical, mental, or emotional well-being is a threat to the voice.

While historical writings make plain that teachers have always been interested in how the vocal mechanism works, it is only in the second half of this century that technology has allowed scientists to examine the workings of the singing voice in detail. Dissemination to a wider community of the body of knowledge developed by voice scientists in recent decades has only begun recently. Today's teachers of singing were trained as singers before that process began; the majority have never had formal training in singing pedagogy. In many cases, they see the physical skills of voice production as important, but because they see those skills in the context of musical imagination and whole-body use, they assume that these can be acquired through listening, observation, practice, and coaching from an expert trained in the tradition.

In a study of singing teaching in Australian tertiary education institutions (Callaghan, 1998) I investigated teachers' knowledge of voice production, analyzed in relation to breath management, phonation, resonance and articulation, registration, vocal health and control of the voice. The highly experienced teachers interviewed saw a knowledge of voice production as important in allowing singers to perform freely and easily, in maintaining vocal health, and in facilitating control of the voice. While many teachers felt that a knowledge of vocal physiology and acoustics was important for teaching singing, most of them assumed this knowledge could be acquired by studying singing and by performing as a singer. Most acquired knowledge of vocal function through doing, listening, observing, and consulting with colleagues. While they thought scientific information about the voice would be of use to singing teachers, they were concerned that such information might interfere with the hearing and feeling aspects of the art and with helping their students to experience singing as an holistic sensory activity.

Vocal control depends on a complex of fine motor coordinations directed by neurological signals and monitored by a range of external and internal feedback. Feedback may come from external sources such as the response of listeners, or from internal feedback such as hearing, vision, touch, kinesthesia, or proprioception. A major source of control is the singer's sensations of vibration.

It is in this way—through audiation, sensory feedback and mental image—that most singers and teachers of singing understand vocal functioning and control. This is pivotal in understanding the relationship between the voice knowledge of scientists and that of musicians.

## Role Perceptions and Values

The practice of any occupation is mediated by the values and judgements inherent in practitioners' perceptions of themselves, of their relation to the body of knowledge and skills used in the practice of that occupation, of their roles in the institutions that employ them, of their relation to professional training or accrediting bodies, of the day-to-day practice of that occupation, of the occupation's function in society, and (in service occupations) of their role with respect to clients. These perceptions are in turn influenced by practitioners' personal circumstances and interests, their training, their experience, and their current employment. Comparison at a general—and necessarily simplistic—level indicates a marked difference between the values of voice teacher and voice scientist, highlighting the lack of fit between the two roles.

The role perception of singing teachers carries with it particular values through which voice knowledge and approaches to teaching are moderated. It implies particular attitudes to the nature of vocal knowledge and how it is best transmitted. Evidence from interviews (Callaghan, 1998) suggests that voice teachers value artistry and individual expression. They value "knowing how" over "knowing that" and assume the oral transmission of knowledge. They emphasize experiential, holistic, sense-based learning. Voice teaching is caring and communicative. It deals with the soma.

Voice scientists, on the other hand, value the technical and technological. They value "knowing that" over "knowing how" and assume the written transmission of knowledge. They emphasize experimental, reason-based learning, which may often be fragmented. Voice science is experimental and rigorous. It deals with the body.

## Craft Knowledge

Bensman and Lilienfeld contended that

> major "habits of mind", approaches to the world, or in phenomenological terms, attitudes towards everyday life, and specialized attitudes, are extensions of habits of thought that emerge and are developed in the practice of an occupation, profession, or craft. We emphasize craft since we focus upon the methods of work, techniques, methodologies, and the social arrangements which emerge in the practice of a profession as being decisive in the formation of world views. (1991, p. xv)

They identified as indigenous to an occupation "an autonomy in the development of craft technique, attitudes towards materials and media, and the development of skill and virtuosity" which give it "distinct and peculiar characteristics of its own" (p. xvi). Bensman and Lilienfeld defined the artistic attitude as one that attempts to create an image of the world in such a way that it can be experienced directly, intuitively, emotionally, and "naively" (p. 5). Important in this world view is a consciousness of and pride in highly developed technique, but a concealing of this technique in an apparent spontaneity, one of the elements by which a great performer is judged (p. 6). There is nothing in such a world view that predisposes practitioners in the arts to take an interest in the sciences, even where scientific knowledge is relevant to their work.

It is this artistic "habit of mind" that I saw in the respondents to my survey of singing teachers in Australian tertiary institutions (Callaghan, 1998). It was clear that respondents identified themselves as singers. That is, they saw themselves primarily as performing artists and identifed with the techniques, attitudes, and skills of musical performers, rather than with those of teachers. Hence their priorities were in developing in their students a whole-body sensation of singing that works at the behest of the imagination and inner ear to meet the demands of musical performance. They felt that to achieve that, a teacher needed experiential knowledge of singing technique, together with a knowledge of vocal repertoire and style, and a knowledge of the main languages of the international repertory of classical vocal music—English, French, German, and Italian. Many of them also saw knowledge of related areas such as body use, acting, and performance-skills enhancement as important. The acquisition and maintenance of knowledge in all these fields represents a major commitment and has a daily relevance; such relevance is not always obvious to teachers in relation to voice science.

## Professional Knowledge

As Donald Schön (1983, 1987) pointed out, the view of professional knowledge implemented by the majority of institutions of higher learning is based on a model of Technical Rationality derived from the long tradition of Positivist thought:

> According to the model of Technical Rationality—the view of professional knowledge which has most powerfully shaped both our thinking about the professions and the institutional relations of research, education, and practice—professional activity consists in instrumental problem solving made rigorous by the application of scientific theory and technique. (1983, p. 21)

The systematic knowledge base of a profession, he says, "is thought to have four essential properties. It is specialized, firmly bounded, scientific, and standardized" (1983, p. 23). Schön sees this last feature as particularly important in relating the profession's knowledge base to its practice (i.e., professionals apply standardized knowledge to particular problems).

This scientific model of professional knowledge is alien to the artistic models held by most singing practitioners. Because they derive their knowledge of voice from their own experience as singers and then apply that knowledge to the particular problems of individual students, many practitioners do not have a concept of a scientific, standardized knowledge of voice. For most of us, our model of voice is performance-related: Our training and experience are in the world of musical performance and our teaching is directed toward that world.

In that world of musical performance, practitioners regard voice as a subject of study in the same way that trumpet or violin are subjects of study. Musicians apply technical facility on their instrument to playing music (or in this case singing music). They then combine the ability to play or sing with a range of musical knowledge and performance skills in the world of musical performance. It is not surprising, then, that some teachers of singing view scientific knowledge of voice as irrelevant, or uncongenial, or too difficult to understand.

## Voice Knowledge

In order to teach vocal technique effectively, it is necessary to understand how the voice works. The puzzle is what "to understand" means in this context. Are practitioners' understandings of vocal technique, learned through their own singing study and performance experience, sufficient for teaching? If a teacher understands through sensation and is able to convey this to the student, is this adequate? While in some cases such an approach may work, given the wide-ranging demands of professional music making today and the context of contemporary education, with its emphasis on economic and educational accountability, this approach is inadequate. It is dependent on the level of understanding—in one mode only—of the teacher and on the teacher's ability to convey this understanding—again, in one mode only—to the student. Even if such an approach does work, it is doubtful whether it is the most efficient approach for all students and for all musical styles. It is usually a slow approach; depending on the student's innate abilities and learning style and the teacher's level of technical competence, it may also be ineffective.

In the preface to *The Relevance of Education*, Jerome Bruner wrote: "I confess I am puzzled ... about the relationship between knowledge as detached (competence?) and knowledge as a guide to purposeful action (performance?)" (1972, p. 16). An understanding of this relationship is essential in approaching the professional education of singing teachers. I propose that competence and performance exist only in relation to each other: Competence is the sum of skills needed for performance, and performance is not possible without competence. This is supported by Reid's assertion that "there is an essential interplay between reflective thinking (which is discursive) and direct intuitive experiences: they need each other" (1986, p. xi). Although vocal technique needs to be felt, there is no reason why it cannot be verbally explained, and no reason why the content of that knowledge cannot be related to the content of voice science knowledge. As Bruner went on to say, "It can also be said of knowledge that, though it is constrained by the very mode of its expression, it can be expressed in various modes" (p. 16).

Many teachers are concerned that if they become too analytical about vocal technique, it will destroy students' ability to learn "by feel." There seem to be two confusions here, a confusion of the teacher's state of mind with the student's, and an assumption that intuitive and analytic ways of knowing are antithetical.

> What then of analysis? Does it really force intuitive knowledge out, is holistic response inevitably left behind? . . . Not necessarily. We must remember that analysis has two complementary definitions. On the one hand analysis is sometimes pulling things apart to find the separate elements, the component parts. . . . On the other hand analysis identifies general principles that may link and underlie individual phenomena. (Swanwick, 1994, p. 31)

Identification of general principles is surely important for both teacher and student. Swanwick (1994) suggested picturing "sensation, intuitive knowledge and what Croce calls logical knowledge as a cumulative continuum, with intuitive knowledge as the bridge between the others, a link made of dynamic forms, images, representations of many types" (1994, pp. 30–31). In order to perform efficiently a whole-body task, one needs an objective, an overview of the task, a knowledge of the component parts, a knowledge of how they fit together, and a system of cueing, such that one activity automatically cues the next. It is the teacher's overview of the task, combining intuitive knowledge, and logical knowledge—the "knowing how" and "knowing that" of singing—and how these modes of knowing are linked in representations of many types that allows construction of an "explanatory model" of voice (Bruner, 1972, p. 16) to assist the student's learning. The difficulty is that teachers who identify themselves primarily as singers, although they are well aware that teaching singing is not just a matter of imparting discrete items of knowledge or technique, do not see it as their responsibility to construct explanatory models.

> Even at the level of "knowing how"—the psycho-motor technical management of an instrument—there are insights to be won into how we actually learn complex skills and sensitivities, gaining control over sound materials. The simple view of what happens would be to assume that a skilled action . . . is the result of tying together into one bundle a number of smaller technical bits into a larger whole, rather like making a broom or a peg rug. But do we really build up a technique from individual bristles, from atoms of muscular behaviour? The element of truth in this is rather small and needs a massive correction. Above all the performance of a skill requires a *plan*, a blueprint, a *schema*, an action pattern. (Swanwick, p. 144)

However, in order to be able to construct an explanatory model for the student, the teacher needs both intuitive and analytic knowledge. Teachers' concern about being "too analytical" involves confusion of what a teacher needs to do with what a student needs to do. Forming a plan is helped by the use of metaphors, mental images, and mind pictures of the action, but teachers are not always aware that the images need to belong to the student and to be linked to the physical realities of the task: "In developing images of action a student is learning how to manage music, becoming autonomous, learning how to learn" (Swanwick, 1994, p. 146).

Likewise, the technical vocabulary of singing teaching needs to be clear and consistent. Concern over the terminology of singing pedagogy has been expressed at many voice meetings in recent years. While a concern with the individual learning needs of students is important, and the development of individual artistic expression is essential, differences in terminology create confusion. Moreover, even where singing teachers may share an understanding of a particular term, a more objective terminology that relates physical function to logic in pedagogical use is needed to facilitate cross-disciplinary communication.

### Professional Education of Singing Teachers

A flexible model of professional education for singing teachers needs to take account of both the craft knowledge currently employed by practitioners in skill teaching and the voice knowledge accumulated through experimental and qualitative research. It needs to take into account the clients of the singing teaching profession and the setting in which their work will be done. Schön advocated that

> university based professional schools should learn from such deviant traditions of education for practice as studios of art and design, conservatories of music and dance, athletics coaching, and apprentice-

ship in the crafts, all of which emphasize coaching and learning by doing. Professional education should be redesigned to combine the teaching of applied science with coaching in the artistry of reflection-in-action. (1987, p. xii)

The "deviant tradition" of singing teaching already incorporates the best of coaching and learning by doing. I propose that a solid basis of content could be incorporated by adopting some aspects of the traditional applied science model in which practitioners learn the body of knowledge of the discipline and how to apply it to particular professional problems. Implementation of such a model relies on respect for the professional orientation of singing teachers as artists preparing students for musical performance. That is, skills teaching needs to be based on cognitive knowledge, and voice knowledge needs to be acquired in a way that serves the learning-by-doing orientation of the profession.

It is no longer adequate for practitioners to base their teaching solely on the directives that were used in their own training, or that they have heard used by famous singers in master classes, or on the personal imagery that has worked for them in their own singing. The directives may not be well based in physical function or vocal acoustics, and the images may not suggest the appropriate coordination to the student. This approach may well be ineffective; at the very least, it is likely to be inefficient. Moreover, it may well be deficient in imparting some essential skills such as those needed to prevent vocal damage.

Adoption of an approach that takes into account the findings of voice science will have various benefits. First, it will eliminate much trial-and-error teaching and will lead to more consistent and predictable results in less time than more traditional methods do. Second, it will enable practitioners to deal with a wider range of singing styles and student requirements than can be accomplished with the traditional methods, whose roots are in the bel canto tradition. Third, it will provide a secure basis for the diagnosis and correction of technical problems. Fourth, it will better equip teachers to teach singing practices based on optimum function and safe voicing, thus reducing the risk that students will develop habits that could cause undue fatigue, produce less than optimum results, or perhaps cause vocal damage. Fifth, it will promote development of standard terminology for the physical skills of singing, thus greatly assisting communication of teachers with students, with other teachers and with other voice professionals. Finally, it will provide a basis for assessing the competing claims and counter-claims of different approaches to singing, both contemporary and historical.

There are signs that these advantages are coming to be more widely appreciated by singing teachers, and the findings of voice science will come to have a much greater influence on the profession than they do at present. Conversely, voice scientists are displaying greater awareness of the relevance to their discipline of the craft knowledge of singing teachers. Such developments will benefit not only both professions, but ultimately everyone—teachers, scientists, executants, and listeners alike—with a serious interest in the art of singing.

## References

Bensman, J., & Lillienfeld, R. (1991). Craft and consciousness. *Occupational technique and the development of world images* (2nd ed.) (Communication & Social Order Series). New York: Aldine de Gruyter.

Bruner, J. (1972). *The relevance of education*. London: Allen & Unwin.

Callaghan, J. (1998). Singing teachers and voice science—An evaluation of voice teaching in Australian tertiary institutions. *Research Studies in Music Education, 10,* 25–41.

Reid, L. A. (1986). *Ways of understanding and education*. London: Heinemann Educational.

Schön, D. A. (1983). *The reflective practitioner: How professionals think in action*. New York: Basic Books.

Schön, D. A. (1987). *Educating the reflective practitioner: Toward a new design for teaching and learning in the professions*. San Francisco: Jossey-Bass.

Swanwick, K. (1994). *Musical knowledge. Intuition, analysis and music education*. London: Routledge.

Titze, I. R. (1994). *Principles of voice production*. Englewood Cliffs, NJ: Prentice Hall.

# AUTHOR INDEX

# SUBJECT INDEX

## A

Abdomen. *See* breath management (abdomen, diaphragm, rib cage), posture, spine
abdominal muscles, 38, 40, 42–43
abdominal pressure, 37
acoustic characteristics of good singing, 77–79
airflow
  breath management and, 31, 32, 43–45, 46
  phonation and, 53
  register change and, 91–92
  singer's formant and, 70–71
  subglottal pressure, tradeoff with, 43
allergies. *See* vocal health
*appoggio* technique, 39
articulation. *See* resonance and articulation
aryepiglottic sphincter, 70, 72, 75
arytenoid cartilages, 68
asthma. *See* vocal health
audiation, 17
audition and auditory system, 16–17

## B

bel canto teaching tradition
  breakdown of assumptions, 6–9
  breath management, phonation, registration, resonance and vocal health in, 3–5

development, assumptions, approach and influence, 1–6
  *see also appoggio* technique, singing pedagogy
"belly-in" and "belly-out." *See under* posture
belting. *See* twang
body and soma, 15–16, 114
body type, 38, 45 (*see also* gender)
breath management, 31–48
  abdomen and, 33–34, 36–39, 40, 42–43, 44
  abdominal pressure and, 37
  airflow, 31, 32, 43–45, 46
  *appoggio* technique, 39
  bel canto masters and, 3–5
  body type and, 38, 45
  chest wall and, 33–34
  diaphragm and, 32–36, 38, 47
  function and characteristics in singing, 19, 31–32
  glottis and, 40, 41
  laryngeal control and, 41, 43–45
  lung volume and pressure and, 31, 42, 43–45
  major voice science findings, 111
  phonation and, 44–45
  posture and, 36–38, 47
  rib cage and, 33–34, 36, 38, 40, 42, 44, 47, 52
  singing pedagogy and, 45–48
  support, 39–43, 44, 111
  vocal instrument and, 19–21
breathiness, 36, 43, 53, 54